FLYING SOLO

Barbara Cropsey Moody

Flying Solo

Barbara Cropsey Moody

All rights reserved. Printed in the United States of America. No part of this book may be reproduced in any manner whatsoever without written permission except in the case of brief quotations embodied in critical articles and reviews.

Copyright © 2017 Barbara Cropsey Moody

First Edition December 2017

ISBN 978-1-943887-56-9

Park Place Publications
Pacific Grove, California
parkplacepublications.com

Bob Moody, affectionately known as "Coot."

Preface

I write to record what I love in the face of loss. I write because it makes me less fearful of death. I write as an exercise of pure joy. I write so that my children, grandchildren, great grandchildren will know me, now and after I'm gone. To let them know they will always have my love and to tell them of the life I have lived.

We were retired. We had time at last to do so many things; travel, learn to play golf, and dance. We would dance, holding each other close, into old age together and then, the music stopped.

A cruel brain tumor caused my handsome partner to lose his balance. We tried to dance on, but it just didn't work. But we could hold hands. It was good, but not as good as dancing.

 Chapter One

The Beginning of the End

January 1998

We were on a small island off the Barrier Reef of Australia. The sun was shining, the palm trees swaying. The hotel had prepared a delicious picnic lunch of lobster tails and crab claws, among many delicious other things, and we were rowed out in a little tin rowboat to a tiny island where we would be the only ones there for the day. How perfectly idyllic. After lunch I found a shady tree to sit under with my watercolors to try to capture this scene on paper. My husband Bob would snorkel in the warm waters within my sight. A half-hour or so later, I saw him trying to walk out of the water. He kept falling, and when he finally made it ashore, his knees were bleeding from being cut on coral. This was surprising, as Bob was an excellent swimmer. He swam competitively in high school and college. At our condo in Poipu Beach on Kauai, he would swim a mile each day between two coral reefs.

Something was wrong.

We went on from the Barrier Reef to the Australian Open tennis matches in Melbourne. It was difficult for Bob to negotiate the stairs leading into the stadium. A telegram from our daughter Robin informing us that both my parents were in hospitals in Florida ended our vacation. We went directly to Florida. At my parents' home, Bob was bumping into walls and falling frequently. We stayed six weeks, until my parents were stabilized, and then headed home to Pebble Beach, CA.

Bob saw our doctor the next day, and he ordered an MRI on Bob's brain. A benign tumor was discovered wrapped around his brain stem. It had set up a cyst within his brain, causing pressure and thus the imbalance. We were referred to Mitchell Berger at UCSF, a neurosurgeon. He operated on Bob's brain, removing the cyst, but felt it unwise to touch the tumor.

• • •

Bob at his 75th birthday party in our home.

 Chapter Two

My Life as a Caregiver

This was the beginning of a sixteen-year battle to have a normal life, each year bringing greater decline to a man who had always been so strong and athletic. This was the beginning of my life as a caregiver, the best and the hardest job I've ever had, and one that became more time-consuming as time went on.

The night following his brain surgery, I could sense Bob was frightened. I asked if I could spend the night with him in his room. They brought in a reclining chair for me. During the night, Bob complained of being cold. No help came when we pressed his button, so I went down the empty hall, opening doors until I found one with blankets. Sometimes you just have to take matters into your own hands.

Six weeks of radiation were prescribed following the operation. We arranged to spend time with our son in San Francisco and our daughter in Piedmont, interspersed with time at the hotel in San Francisco, so as not to wear out our welcome in either child's home.

The radiation was draining. Our anniversary occurred during this time, and Bob was determined we would go to dinner at a very special restaurant. The poor guy almost fell asleep over his dinner.

Of course, I had taken over the driving, and on my birthday, Bob took me to a hat shop to buy a chauffeur's cap as a joke, more or less. It came in handy on "Bad Hair Days."

After a while, we were able to take trips again, including a memorable one to Africa on safari with Abercrombie and Kent in 2001, the year of our 50th wedding anniversary. Previously we had traveled on our own, just the two of us, deciding where we'd stay and go all on our own. This time we put ourselves in the hands of a trusted travel group and toured Kenya, Tanzania, Zimbabwe, and South Africa. It was wonderful. Bags were taken care of, and easily accessible rooms were arranged for. We took out travel insurance, including Medevac.

It turned out to be an outstanding experience. We saw all the "Big Five" animals in the wild: elephants, hippos, rhinos, lions, and giraffes. We danced with the natives, stood looking out at Victoria Falls holding umbrellas over our heads, and made new friends.

While Bob's balance was better after the removal of the cyst, it was not perfect. I referred to him as a member of the "Frequent Faller's Club." He was persuaded to use a cane. With that and holding my arm on the other side, he was a bit more stable, but when he did go down, he took me with him. No fun, I can assure you.

We loved to dance, and went to dances frequently, but it wasn't possible anymore. Bob also gave up tennis and swimming. The last sport he gave up was golf. His foursome was very patient as they watched him teeter as he teed-off, and helped him find the balls he hit into the rough.

We saw a neurologist who said he drank too much, which caused the imbalance. I assured her that I had known him since he was 18, and had never seen him drunk. He thanked me for "sticking up for him."

In 2003, he had a triple-bypass at a hospital that specialized in heart surgery. This hospital had a small four-bedroom ranch house adjacent to its parking lot, where relatives could stay without charge. We drove up the night before the operation. I moved into the guest house for five days and was able to spend all day each day with Bob. I had my meals at the hospital cafeteria. When Bob was able, we walked the hospital corridors together, and eventually drove back home.

Blood tests now revealed that Bob had Non-Hodgkin's lymphoma, and we added an oncologist to the list of doctors we must see. To his credit, he prolonged Bob's life for another 11 years.

Lymphoma is a cancer of the blood. The platelets are greatly reduced, thus lowering the immune system. It was important to avoid people who might spread germs. We asked family and friends not to visit if they were sick. We became, in many ways, more isolated than we had ever been.

We decided to take bridge lessons as an activity we could do together sitting down. At the class we met another couple our age with similar interests. Both men were retired lawyers and both women had careers in health-related fields. After the classes we decided to play at each other's homes twice a week, two hours each Monday and Thursday afternoons. We all looked forward to those games, not really caring who won. It was the sociability that made it fun.

On Bob's birthday, shortly after our 60th wedding anniversary, our three children gave Bob a walker. He didn't want to use it, although it was apparent to everyone that he needed it. After a few months of it sitting in the garage, he took it for a spin and declared it helpful. Gradually, we added two more in the house, and a third in the car trunk, plus a chair elevator for our two-story home. Now Bob could go from walker to elevator to walker to get around the house.

We had a pleasant daily routine: having breakfast (Bob often preparing it) then taking our second cups of coffee to the library to read the papers, then seeing if we had any doctor's appointments that day.

By now we had gotten a handicap sign for the car, which was a great help. We looked for stores, restaurants, and even barber shops with easy access. On days when we went to the barber's together, we'd pick up sandwiches at the same shopping center, then drive to a pull-out on 17-Mile Drive where there was a picnic table just steps away from where I could park the car. I kept a safari hat in the trunk for Bob to protect his fair skin and keep the sun out of his eyes.

He now had macular degeneration. Never having been a football fan, I now watched every game to tell Bob the score, what quarter it was, and how much time was left in the quarter. I became a fan. We bought playing cards with larger numbers for our bridge games.

In the mornings, I read the headlines to Bob and he chose the stories he wanted to hear. There were two stocks he always wanted the quotes on.

Because his eyesight was failing, he was unable to write legibly, so I took over the checkbook.

It was often exasperating for him to turn over so many things that he had always controlled to someone of lesser intellect (me), and I had to constantly remind myself how it must be for him, and not return anger with anger.

We'd had season tickets to the symphony for many years. The parking became difficult, and getting him in and out with the walker. He would get restless and want to leave by intermission, and so we gave it up.

We went out to restaurants for lunch occasionally, as it was easier to manage in daylight. I designated Saturday night our date night. We stayed at home and I made martinis for us, and grilled steak. We both looked forward to that.

In 2008, Bob decided we would take a cruise around the world, obviously a bucket-list item. We left in January and returned at the end of April. It wasn't easy, but we did it.

There were always crew members to get you up and down gangplanks, and in and out of launches. In some places, we had to ward off vendors or beggars. That was up to me. Bob couldn't stay up after 7:30 pm, so we went to the early dinner seating. We missed most of the entertainment and parties planned for later in the evenings.

One evening we were anchored in the harbor at Hong Kong, and there was a spectacular light show above the city that we could view from the deck. I secured a deck chair for Bob and blankets in a chest on deck to put over him, and we enjoyed the lights together.

Whenever we traveled by air, I made sure we both had wheelchairs coming and going. I was able to walk, but not fast enough to keep up with Bob's wheelchair pushers, so as the old saying goes, "If you can't beat 'em, join 'em."

Let's talk about bars. Not the kind that serves drinks, the kind you can grab to help you get up or give you a sense of security. We started out with them in the shower and around the toilets, and then Bob thought of more places where they'd be helpful. So you could say he spent his time going from bar to bar. It was a good idea.

● ● ●

*Moorea, after Coot's haircut in Papeete, Tahiti.
Norwegian Liner* Amsterdam *is in the background.*

Help!

Of course you will need help. For us, visits from our children and grandsons were the best. They not only picked up our spirits, but were always so helpful: changing light bulbs, moving furniture, etc. Of course the rugs all had to be rolled up, cleaned, and put away. Furniture had to be rearranged to allow the walkers to pass through.

As time passed it became apparent that we would need more help as Bob could not be left alone in case he fell. I called the daughter of a friend who had need of help for 15 years, to get the name of the agency her mother used. It turned out to be an excellent way to find reliable help. They were with us when needed until the end.

The help that meant the most to both of us was the help

from our children. They usually came on weekends, holidays, and our birthdays, which of course made those times special. They also made it possible for us to get places that would have been impossible on our own.

Bob loved to go to Costco. I would get him a shopping cart in the parking lot, and he could enter the store looking like any other customer. Of course, he got a lot of things we really didn't need, but so what? He was happy.

● ● ●

Bob

Fair-skinned with strawberry blonde hair that, as he aged, became a soft blonde. I loved his hair. I also loved his hands. Slim fingers, firm but not rough. Arms and legs covered in the same curly strawberry blonde hair.

As a young student and then lawyer: impeccably dressed in shirts, ties and business suits. *In retirement:* khaki trousers, polo shirts and cashmere sweaters. The same Ferragamo shoes he wore for 20 years. If he liked something he stuck with it.

He liked to eat on time and had a good appetite. After he retired, he also liked to cook and, like everything else he did, he did it very well, breakfasts especially.

Bob showed very little emotion about anything. The only time I remember him so angry that he was about to haul off and hit someone was when Peter lost the dog at Soldier Field. I intervened by saying we had just spent $1600 on orthodontia on him, so please don't punch him in the face. He never cried or showed over-enthusiasm. I guess you could say he was calm.

He loved to travel, to participate in and watch sports. He liked ice cream, pumpkin pie, chocolate éclairs, opera and watching the ocean. When I met him, I thought he was not only handsome but interesting and charming. We could have a good time without spending much money. He had good manners and ambition. He tried to teach me to swim, play tennis and bridge. I was a disappointment in all, but I was always willing to try whatever he suggested, and so we married. He was totally loyal, completely trustworthy, and we worked together to have a pleasant life with three wonderful children and grandchildren.

There were just five words I wish he had been able to say more often: "I love you" and "thank you."

He liked money. He was good at saving, investing, and keeping track of it with meticulous spreadsheets and record folders. He was thrifty, but would spend on things he deemed worthwhile. He drank "Two-buck Chuck" but took us on a four-month trip around the world. He loved to shop at Costco and even invested in it when the stock was $10 a share. He gave generously to brain tumor research at UCSF. His name is on the wall with other major contributors.

Bob provided me with a lifestyle I could never had imagined: travels all over the world; beautiful homes in lovely communities; playing tennis and golf; lessons in art, writing and languages; swimming and skiing. And over the course of it all, I thanked him over and over and always told him I loved him.

● ● ●

Serendipity

We decided to go to Toasties in Pacific Grove one Sunday morning, continuing our quest to find the perfect *huevos rancheros*. The parking place we were able to find was at least half a block away. I got out the walker, helped Bob out of the car and up the curb to the sidewalk. At our usual leisurely pace, a young couple passed us. By the time we got to the door and waiting area all the seats had been taken there, but the couple who had passed us insisted we take their seats. When their name was called for a table, they again insisted we take their turn. When their turn followed, they were seated not far from us. Toasties' *huevos rancheros* were indeed good! When I asked for the check, we were told it had been taken care of. I looked over at the couple, shook my finger, and said, "you shouldn't have done this." They just smiled.

When we left, I helped Bob into the Mercedes with the Pebble Beach shield, and they passed us waving from their pickup truck. What a lovely way to start a Sunday morning.

The Dog

There came a time when travel just became too difficult. We had traveled the world together and separately for years. Now it was over. I felt we needed something to give us another interest outside of health problems. How about a dog?

Bob said, "No way, Jose. No dog." So of course I started looking for one. An ad appeared in the local paper with a picture of a dog named "CoCo." It invited people to meet CoCo in front of a pet shop on Saturday.

I was there early with my friend Mary, a dog lover. CoCo was late, but sitting on the lap of one of the adoption representatives was an adorable little blonde dog wearing a scarf that said "Adopt Me." I asked if I could walk her on her leash. She walked well, didn't tug. I guess you could say it was love at first sight.

Sugar, the sweetest dog in the whole world!

By the time CoCo arrived, it was too late. I'd fallen for "Trixie." I did want to change her name, though, as Trixie sounded like a name a hooker might have. My dog would have a more lady-like name, like "Sugar."

It was agreed that I could have Trixie/Sugar if my house could pass inspection the next morning. I said nothing to Bob about this. Sunday morning came, and after breakfast and reading the papers, Bob said, "Let's go to Costco around 11:00. We can have lunch. I'll buy you a hot dog."

I replied, "It will have to be later because someone is coming to see the house at 11:00."

"Why does anyone want to see our house?"

"Because we're getting a dog."

"Oh no," followed by silence.

A knock on the door and Ellie arrived with Sugar, who went directly to Bob and licked his fingers while looking at him with those big brown eyes. He was hooked. Our house and yard passed inspection. We had a dog!

As things turned out, Bob spent more time talking to Sugar than he did to me, and when I took Sugar for walks twice a day, it became a social experience. We got to know all the dogs in the neighborhood and their owners. What a blessing that little dog was for both of us.

When it became apparent that the end was near, Bob's oncologist had suggested it was time for hospice, something I had been putting off facing for years, our wonderful son Bill came to be with us for that last six weeks. I had moved Bob to a bedroom downstairs to make things easier, as it was closer to the laundry (there was a lot of that, including sheets) and the kitchen. I slept with him in that room, but was up every two hours to tend to his needs.

When Bill arrived, we decided that we could go all day but

not all night as well. We made arrangements for the agency to send a man to spend the nights, change the bed and give Bob a shower in the morning. Raul was our guy, ever cheerful, energetic, and so caring. He became part of the family.

Bill's idea was that we go for a drive along the ocean everyday, and have lunch at some place with a view. We traveled from Monterey to Big Sur, making each day something special.

When Bob became too weak to make the effort, our wonderful daughter Robin joined us for that last 10 days. She had been faithful in coming so many weekends as well over the years.

Hospice set Bob up with a hospital bed and Robin would come in with her computer on the other side of the room to keep Bob company. She was preparing to start a new job as Chief Financial Officer of a craft brewery.

One afternoon, Bob said to her, "I guess I'll never taste your beer." He had given up eating and was limiting himself to water through a straw.

Robin replied, "Of course you will. There's a six-pack in the fridge,"

"Well, can I have it now?"

"No, you'll have to wait until 5:00."

At the appointed hour, Robin poured him a little in a glass and asked if he'd like a straw. He said, "No," he'd take a full glass, no straw. So we raised the hospital bed to a sitting position and gave him his glass.

Robin, Bill and I joined him with a toast to what a great guy he was. Bill began to tell a funny story, and we all started laughing. Bob's face was flush, and he looked as handsome and happy as the day I met him.

Somehow, we knew this would be his last night, and we

decided to cancel Raul and take care of him ourselves. We told him how much he was loved, and that we understood if he had to leave. It was hard to let go, but he really wanted to move on to his next adventure. Early the next morning his breathing stopped. The three of us went out into the garden where dawn was breaking and the clouds were tinged with pink.

"Goodbye Coot. We know you're up there watching over us." After 63 years of marriage and 16 years of ill health, it was not easy to say goodbye, but we did our best to take care of you and to give you a good send off.

● ● ●

 Chapter Three

Flying Solo: My Life as a Widow

The first flight I took alone was to Kiahuna, our condo in Kauai. My son Bill was there to meet me at the airport in Lihue. We spent two weeks there. Bill was a wonderful guide, taking us to many places I had not seen in the more than 40 years we had been coming to the island. This was a trip immediately following my husband's death.

Bill and I had been caring for Bob together for the last six weeks, and it was time to rest and recharge our batteries. Everyday we thought of Bob and how much he had enjoyed this place, how he swam every day from reef to reef until he'd reached a mile. The Mai Tais and barbecues and listening to Hawaiian

On the beach at Kiahuna, Hawaii.

music. It was a real healing experience after a difficult time of letting go and saying goodbye to a partner of over 63 years.

● ● ●

My brother Jeff has invited me to visit him and his family in Pensacola, Florida. We plan to attend a performance of the Pensacola Symphony on March 7th, a Saturday evening. On the following Monday, I will fly to Palm Beach to visit Marge Odeen, an old friend. I'm so excited the night before departure that I hardly sleep. A friend picks me up at 8:00 am to catch the Monterey Airbus to San Jose Airport for a flight to Houston, then after a brief layover, on to Pensacola. But the flight from Houston to Pensacola has been cancelled with no hope of a flight the next day, so I book a flight to Mobil, Alabama, only 73 miles away.

But first I must locate my suitcase. This takes two hours. It is almost 2:00 am and I am spending the night sitting up at the Houston Airport. It's pretty much deserted at this hour, but I've camped out on one of two upholstered chairs in the whole airport, so things could be worse, but not much worse. They say things will open up again between 4:00 am-5:00 am, only two more hours to go. Checking the departure charts, it appears that a plane may leave for Pensacola at 7:24 am. I hope this is true and that I will be on it. Sleep is highly over-rated, although I suppose I will eventually hit the wall from lack of it. I have a book to read and a bag of dried apricots and nuts.

Two gentlemen join me in the area. One an army vet who served in Iraq as well as Afghanistan, but is now in private business, anxious to get home to his family in Oklahoma City. I found his take on Afghanistan and the Taliban most interesting. The other fellow had just missed his connecting flight to

Guadalajara, Mexico. A representative of Hewlett-Packard, he was trying to return home from a trip that had taken him from India, to Paris and London. More interesting conversation on travel and electronics. He shared a chocolate bar from Paris with me and I shared my nuts with him. And so the long night passed.

Robin called me on my cell phone, and seemed a little concerned about my safety. I assured her I was a "big girl" and could take care of myself, and actually I couldn't have been safer with my two guardians.

Finally 4:30 came, and the ticket counter opened. I am at the front of the line to change my ticket from Mobile back to Pensacola. Success!

I'm on my way and Jeff is at the Pensacola Airport with a big hug and a red rose to welcome me.

Their new home in Pace, a suburb of Pensacola, is lovely. On a quiet cul-de-sac surrounded by woods, it is fresh and so up-to-date. Beautiful kitchen, dining area, and family room with a huge TV and comfortable seating. There is also a formal dining room at the front of the house. Lee, Jeff, and Matt each have a suite consisting of bedroom, bath and sitting room. I've been given Matt's for my stay, which is most comfortable. Matt is camping out in Jeff's office on a fold-out bed. What a good kid.

Jack is a beautiful, 75-pound black Labrador, and we have taken a mutual liking to each other. Jack thinks he is a lap dog and loves to cuddle up and give kisses. I have no objection.

On our first afternoon after I get settled, Jeff and I go downtown for lunch at a new restaurant called The Bodacious Olive. Yummy salads. A tour of the art museum and then parts of historic downtown. Pensacola is really an interesting and historic city, the oldest in the USA. In one of the squares they are gearing up for a barbecue cook-off tomorrow.

On returning home, we find Lee home early from her job. She has a bad cold and we urge her to get to bed and try to shake it, but she insists on making a delicious dinner before doing so. Jeff introduces me to Netflix and we watch *House of Cards* and then to bed.

On Friday, we have a lazy morning. Jeff of course gets phone calls connected with work, and I love to hear how easily he answers each one, solving the caller's problem in a matter of minutes. Lee has wisely decided to stay in bed and nurse the cold. Jeff and I go to the Air Museum on the base at Pensacola. We have lunch at the Cubi Club in the museum, which is a replica of a club at Cubic Bay in the Philippines, WWII era. Fun, and great clam chowder in a bread bowl. We decide to see an Imax movie, *The Magic of Flight*, featuring the Blue Angels, and feeling like you are flying the plane. It is spectacular.

Afterwards, we tour the museum, seeing planes from every

era starting with one of the Wright Brothers'. Perhaps the most interesting parts for me were the replicas of a WWII base in the Pacific where there is the same field desk that I use at home, the one Colonel Earnest Smith used. The other being "On the Home Front," bringing back memories of ration stamps, big Hershey bars for a nickel, wringer washing machines, old radios, etc. What a perfect time capsule. Loved the museum. We do some errands on the way home, discover Lee feeling much better, and enjoy another delicious dinner together, followed by TV.

I should mention that during a nice visit with Matt on the day I arrived, just the two of us, I asked him to explain the significance of his tattoos. He has sleeves on both arms. Matt is a man with artistic talents as well as interests. One arm is done in Japanese motifs, as he is a great admirer of Japanese art, as am I. The other arm is Native American. Both arms are beautifully done, and it was interesting to me to find out about them.

Saturday is here and we decide to go to Jaco's for a mid-day meal. We sit outside on their deck with a view of the beautiful yachts in the harbor, Pensacola Bay in the background. We hear the sound of horns being blown to celebrate the Jewish Festival of Purim, and out on a pier, a wedding is going on. Pensacola is, as Bill would say, "a happening place," and at Jaco's we seem to be right in the middle of things.

On to Fort Pickens, an old fort built by slaves during the Civil War to protect Pensacola. The canons were most impressive, and I can see why no ships got through.

After coffee and cheesecake, Jeff and I take off for downtown and a performance of *Don Quixote* by the Pensacola Symphony. It was marvelous! A full house in the red velvet cushioned theatre. Pensacola is bustling on a Saturday night.

We were having a leisurely Sunday morning, drinking coffee and reading the newspapers, when Jack got out and in his usual bounding, playful Jack way, he knocked over a woman who was visiting next door. Talk about All Hell Breaking Loose. As the woman left to be examined at the hospital, Jeff got out his insurance policies; Lee was close to hysterical. Over-reactions all around.

Finally things settled down enough for Jeff, Matt and I to go for a ride over the bridge along the Pensacola beaches again, in the direction of Alabama. When it becomes less scenic, we turn around and go to the Grand Mariner for a late lunch. Goodbyes to Lee and Matt in the evening, as they'll be going to work early in the morning. Jeff gets me to the airport the next morning, and I am off to my next adventure with Marge Odeen in Palm Beach.

The Odeens reside in a beautiful condo right on the beach at Turtle Bay. Marge has furnished it largely with finds from thrift shops. My kinda girl. She is also helping her son Mark furnish and decorate condos and townhouses he is "flipping." In other words, he buys low, rehabs or remodels, then sells at a profit. Part of my adventure was going along to "spot" for Marge. My greatest find was a desk at Goodwill for $69 along with a round table and four chairs for $49. In between times we checked out a turtle hospital, played bridge, had lunch as well as dinner out with different groups of friends, and saw an absolutely wonderful production of *Les Miserables*. It was an action-packed two days and loads of fun.

The wonderful thing about old friends is you take off from where you left off, 30 years ago. No need for explanations. It is all natural and comfortable. Actually, our "scouting" was very similar to what the two of us started doing together in 1973 when we met at a Welcome Wagon gathering in Lake Forest, Illinois, and discovered we had both bought big old historic houses that needed lots of fixing up as well as furnishings and accessories. We teamed up to go to estate sales and warehouse clearances all over the Chicago area, and succeeded after a few years in creating charming homes. It was like "old times" in Palm Beach—both older—but like the fire house horses: out the door in a flash, in pursuit of bargains. What fun! We still had it. Was I glad I made that trip? You bet I was!

● ● ●

Flying solo is not just about trips. I am alone for the first time in my life. I lived in my parents' home even through my college years, having commuted to school everyday and returning every evening. The day I left that happy house was my wedding day. Somehow I am comfortable alone, although I would not have chosen it. There is time to read as well as write, and most of all, to go out, do what I like without having to consider others. It's a novelty.

There are those who think I should exhibit more sadness,

but I have adjusted to my situation and have no regrets about my life before this. I am cleaning out and giving away things, streamlining my house and life. It actually feels good.

● ● ●

On an overcast rainy day, I'm wearing one of my husband's warm sweaters. It's like a hug from him. I'm also reading the diary he kept on his trek to Mt. Everest with our son Bill. It's as if he was telling me this story all over again, 27 years later.

And then I hear of the earthquake and subsequent avalanches. I know all these places. Bob has taken me there with his diary. What an incredible coincidence.

I call my house "Contentment." The word is on a bronze plaque on the arch over the entrance to the garden. The truth is I am content there. I love my garden and every room in my house. I love the old furniture and artwork. I can think of no other place I'd rather be.

People ask me how I stayed married to the same man for 63 years. I'll relate this to a conversation I had with my son Bill one night after he'd returned from surfing on the Big Sur Coast.

"Isn't it dangerous?" I asked. "Aren't you scared when those big rocks come into view? Don't you want to ditch out?"

Bill's reply: "Sure, but once you commit to your wave, you have to ride it all the way to the beach. Otherwise it could be disastrous."

I rode my wave all the way, and tried to make it the best, most exciting ride of my life. I knew there would only be one.

• • •

Châteauneuf-du-Pape

We had a house in Los Altos Hills in the 60s on two acres of land, which was large enough to permit us to have a horse. We bought a palamino and named him Montana because that was where he was from. All the kids in the neighborhood called him "Montana Moody." As a family we built Montana a two stall barn and a corral, installed an old clawfoot bathtub to hold his water, and supplied him with ample hay. We all enjoyed riding him up into the hills. A bridle path ran right by, in front of our house. Several times a month we raked up the manure, put it in the garbage cans, and took it to the dump.

Fast forward to March 2015, I'm at a swanky private club in Palm Beach, Florida, and my host asks, "May I pour you a glass of wine? It's Châteauneuf-du-Pape."

"Oh yes, I know that wine well."

A long time ago, I was a deaconess at the Congregational Church in Los Altos. One of my responsibilities was to prepare Communion. I had gotten a jug of red wine, something inexpensive like Gallo and left it in the station wagon, as well as a loaf of fresh baked bread. I was cubing the bread into little squares when I heard the car leave the driveway. Bob was taking the manure to the dump, along with the Communion wine. He would not be back before it was time for me to go to church. There was just one thing to do: take several bottles of Bob's Châteauneuf-du-Pape. The best Communion we ever had!

● ● ●

Friends

I didn't know how many good friends I had until I was alone. They have made sure that there is something for me to do every day that takes me out of the house and provides contact with others. I start with aqua aerobics class at the Monterey Sports Center from 8:00-9:00 am. This gets me revved-up and going. On Monday, I go on to the memoir class at the Carmel Foundation. I love to hear others' stories. On other days I play bridge, usually having lunch with the friends I play with. When I get home in the late afternoon I read my mail, pay bills, read two newspapers and part of a book. On the weekends I often go to a movie with a friend, or a flower show, or sometimes the symphony.

Me and my pal, Mary McNamara, on our first day in Florence.

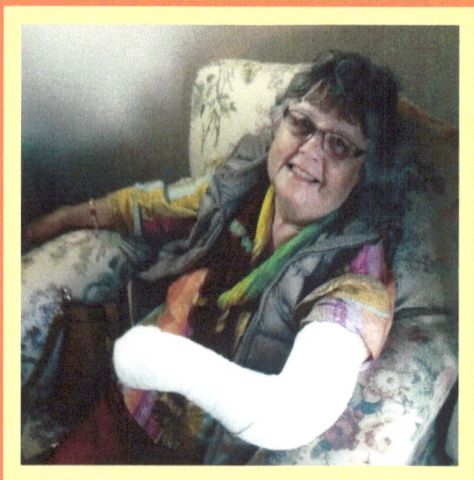

My second day in Florence.

Our last night; signing my cast.

At home I think of Bob, all the things we did together, trips where we purchased so many furnishings in our house: rugs in Turkey and Morocco and Tibet; china, silverware and antiques in England; seashells picked up on beaches all over the world; copper molds in France and Italy; a blow gun acquired from a chief in the Amazon; and of course, pictures of us smiling together everywhere. I truly am a very lucky person. I feel Bob's presence always, so while I am physically alone, I am not lonely.

● ● ●

The Agony and Ecstasy of Tuscany

Florence at last!

Sitting on the balcony at the San Remigio Inn next to the church of San Remigio, whose bells ring faithfully on the half hour.

A plump pouty pigeon has nested in a space between two of the ancient bricks in the wall of the church. When the bells ring, he stops his preening and listens too.

The organ is playing and the choir singing. Dogs barking and shoppers shopping below us. We are in the very heart of the city.

A long day flying over the pole from San Francisco with my dear friend Mary McNamara, a stop in Paris, but we are here now, and it was worth the trouble.

Did I bring enough?

Did I pack too much?

Will I like the group?

Will they like me?

Will my paintings please?

Will they be a flop?

By the weeks end,

All will be revealed.

From lovely San Francisco

To a rainy day in Paris

To the sunny warmth of Italy

A journey to remember!

Tuscany! My God I love Tuscany: the food, the wine and the scenery! The art and old antiquities inspire and amuse me.

In spite of a broken wrist, I carry on and do what I wish. Seeing churches and paintings, eating and drinking red wine. Enjoying the flow of conversation on any number of subjects, none trivial. It is all a diversion from the constant pain and inconvenience of the bulky plaster cast encasing my left arm.

How a glance up at the sky and missing a half step on a terra cotta tile patio changed my life in an instant. Losing my balance, I fall. New friends rush to help.

Someone says, "Get David, he's an orthopedic surgeon."

David takes one look and says, "It's broken. Someone get a splint."

In seconds, a spoon rest from the kitchen arrives with a blue packet of ice and a dishtowel. One of the women takes the beautiful scarf from her neck to serve as a sling. With the help of our Italian hostess we are off to the hospital, Santa Maria Annunciata, some 20 minutes away.

Take a number, wait your turn, x-ray: *fractura*, no English spoken. Operating room. *Fractura* set without anesthesia, excruciating pain, voices in the background shouting, "*Brava Barbara!*" over my screams.

More x-rays. Cast from shoulder to wrist. Ride home at midnight with David, a member of our group who has come to appreciate the art of Tuscany. He was with me in the operating room assuring me it would be alright and checking x-rays. The only English voice I heard. Thank God he was there.

I thought of returning home the next day. David said, "No, try it for a day. See how it goes." So I did. One day followed another, filled with activity and so many helping hands. The nights were most difficult, keeping my roommate Mary awake with the moaning I couldn't help. She never complained, only helped and sympathized.

Beautiful paintings, magnificent churches all described by knowledgeable guides. Rides down winding roads with scenic views of fields of grape vines and olive trees.

It is harvesting time and tractors pull containers filled with grapes. When the going gets rough, I find a seat at a sidewalk café and wait for the group to return from their tour. Then it's back on the bus and on to the next adventure.

● ● ●

Somehow a week passes.

Robin, my daughter, has been notified of my condition, and in her typical efficient fashion, has located the very best hand specialist in San Francisco, who has agreed to see me as soon as I can get to his office after the plane lands. His decision is to operate in a few days and place five pins in my wrist to secure the bones. I stay with Robin in Berkeley. She drives me back and forth to all appointments and takes care of me in every way.

How lucky I have been to have first David Hootnick, my wonderful roommate Mary, all the members of our group, and then Robin to look out for me.

It was a trip I'll never forget, both for the agony and the ecstasy of Tuscany.

● ● ●

Thanksgiving

I'm not fond of turkey, but I do like a party!

My Thanksgiving started on the Tuesday before, when my son Peter arrived to spend the night and take me up to San Francisco the next day for my last doctor's appointment for my now healing broken wrist. We listened to Sirius Radio, featuring Frank Sinatra, and sang along with him.

Everything A-OK with my wrist. The only thing to work on is getting a grip.

My Italian daughter-in-law, Mara, took me shopping and then home to a wonderful gnocchi dinner after one of Peter's perfectly prepared martinis.

The three of us crossed the Bay Bridge to Berkeley and Thanksgiving dinner at Robin and Jim's. The table was beautifully set, the dinner wonderful, and conversation such fun. Robin and Jim gave me their room with the beautiful view of the Bay and the city lights. The rest of the weekend included seeing the movie "Brooklyn," a beautiful love story. I recommend it! And on Sunday evening a performance by the Berkeley Choir at the Claremont Club of Christmas carols and a tree lighting ceremony with lots of children in attendance, all dressed up and suitably impressed by the lights on the tree.

What am I most thankful for? My wonderful, caring, considerate family. Can't you tell?

• • •

It's a rather gloomy Sunday. Rain during the night, cloudy and drizzling in the morning. An email tells me that expected company will have to cancel because of illness. OK. Sunday is the day I look forward to reading the *New York Times*—all of it. After breakfast, that is exactly what I do. Today I am also determined to play the CD player, and following the step-by-step instructions that my grandson Jack has scotch-taped to the cabinet door, I do it! I'm especially interested in playing Willie Nelson's *Stardust* album. Jack gave it to me for Christmas with the note, "Remember that magical night driving back from Will and Malia's wedding, playing this CD and all three of us singing the words to each song?" One of those songs was "September Song." It was almost September that night, the end of August. We didn't know then what little time we had left before Bob would die in November. So the refrains at the end of each verse were more precious than they'd ever been:

As the days dwindle down to a precious few
September, November
And these precious days I'll spend with you

I ate my lunch listening to each song sung in Willie's raspy voice and remembered that magical night and the closeness we all felt. No one can know how many days we have left, so the lesson for all of us may be to make each of them precious.

• • •

Spring was here and it was time to spread Bob's ashes on Lopez Island in the San Juans, on Coot's Island, named for him on our son's property. Coot was Bob's nickname, and he had specified just where on the island he wished his remains to be. Everyone was notified of the date and time and told that they might say a few words if they wished.

Our minister suggested we might want to put flowers down as we sprinkled the ashes, but I didn't like that idea. When I woke on Friday morning, I looked out the window and saw apple trees in blossom and knew that was what we should have. Bill and I went to a nursery and picked out an apple tree. Not just an ordinary apple tree, but one that had four different kinds of apples grafted to its trunk: Fuji, Stanton, Gala, and Ambrosia. It was a complex tree, as Coot had been a complex person. Bill prepared the soil and planted it that afternoon.

A couple of larger Aspen trees on the island had fallen during winter storms, so Bill and his son Nick arranged the trunks for seating adjacent to the new apple tree. Nick had cut a few rounds off the Aspen trunks, and with his chain saw carved out the letters C-O-O-T, and placed them at the base of the apple tree. Over the years they will disintegrate and nourish the tree.

In order of age the children and grandchildren spoke. I could not have been more touched or more proud. Robin outlined the highlights of a brilliant career as well as the care of a loving dad. Bill read from a diary Coot had kept on a Mt. Everest trek that they shared, and told us that regardless of his choice of lifestyle,

Aspen tree rings spell out "COOT" and surround his ashes.

Robin, Bill, Barbara, and Peter.

Malia and Will.

Coot had always been supportive. Peter brought a portable CD player, and played some of Coot's favorite songs: *Cool Water*, *My Life Has Been a Pleasure*, *All Because of You*, and the last of which was the *Washington & Lee Swing*. Pete, my brother Jeff (both alumni) and I sang the words as loud as we could. Coot would have loved it.

Our oldest grandson Will had brought a guitar and his wife Malia brought her ukulele. He recalled an evening on Kauai when he and his brother were little and there with us listening to a Hawaiian radio station from Honolulu. They announced that they would take requests, and the boys urged Bob to call in with his favorite Hawaiian song. About 15 minutes later, a voice came over the airwaves to say, "now for Coot on Kauai we will play the *Carburetor Song*." Will had Googled the words and music, and he and Malia did a fine rendition.

Jack told of Grandpa's encouragement in every sport, and Nick, Solomon, and Marta were equally eloquent in their appreciation of a truly great grandfather. Each boy wore something of Bob's: Will, a sweater; Jack, a Hawaiian shirt; and Nick, a wool plaid shirt.

My brother Jeff and Robin's husband Jim participated, and then David Smith, an old friend of Bill's who would come by whenever we visited to talk to Bob about his travels, got up with what proved to be a large tray wrapped in plastic bags. He had looked out his window that morning and noticed that his peach tree had dropped all its blossoms. He gathered them up and brought them to cover the ashes.

Finally I read a short note I'd written. It said: "Dearest Coot, Thank you for a wonderful life. I will always love you. Babs." I tore it in little pieces and laid them on top. The minister recited that wonderful Irish poem, "May the road come up to greet you, May the wind be at your back." We all left for the house where we toasted Coot with champagne for a life well-lived.

Summer in Pebble Beach, close to the ocean, is often overcast, foggy, drizzly, and after so many of these days, I long for the sun. I know where to find it. It is usually just a few miles away in

Carmel Valley, or sometimes even as close as Costco's parking lot. More often than not I opt for Carmel Valley. I can stop along the way at my favorite nursery and walk up and down the rows of plants and flowers. What a treat! I love it! Then travel on down the road to meet a friend for lunch as long as it's at a place where we can sit outside and bask in the sun. Sun is like nourishment, a tonic. It feeds my soul.

● ● ●

June 30, 2015

On the road again, this time to visit my son Bill and his family on Lopez Island in Puget Sound, Washington. The days are longer here. The son rises at 4:00 am and sets at 10:00 pm. Everything is lush and green. Tall pines, aspen, and redwoods. Bill is building the second half of his house, and his partner has the most fabulous garden filled with flowers, vegetables and herbs.

We eat from the garden: sweet peas, beets and kale. There are Buddhas everywhere. Bill's partner Life Has Meaning is a Buddhist and vegetarian. All the meals are meatless unless we go to a restaurant. My grandson Nick has made a fine bed for me, and Bill has gotten a brand new mattress for me. I feel like a queen.

We have a leisurely breakfast every morning, maybe go to town to do some errands, then back for lunch, followed by a half-hour nap, then reading or writing, and of course watching the house construction. We gather for gin and tonics in the evenings, then dinner. There is also good conversation with the young people; Nick's girlfriend, Gloria, and Solomon, and sometimes Emabet and whoever else drops by and stays for dinner. Right now I'm sitting in a breezeway between the house and bath house, Tibetan prayer flags are fluttering overhead. It's another world.

Of course, we are all looking forward to the 4th of July celebration, two days hence. You'll hear more about that later….

The parade down the main street of Lopez Vilage seemed smaller this year. We staked out our usual spot on the corner just across from the library and watched the floats, tractors, bikes, horses and fire trucks go by. In the evening we packed some things to share at a potluck on a property with its own pond. Kids and some adults swam or kayaked and then gathered around the fire to dry off, warm up, and watch the meat and salmon cook.

Three friends of Nick's camped out on Bill's property with their girlfriends for the weekend. They had all left Lopez after college to find jobs on the mainland. A nice group and very quiet. So another 4th of July passed, and a few days later it was time for me to go home.

The weather this summer has been unusually warm and sunny, like a normal Eastern summer. I bought a little table and chairs with an umbrella to enjoy eating my lunch on the deck outside. It's been very pleasant. Members of the family have come for weekend visits, and Will and Malia even spent their two week vacation with me. That was great. We went to the Bach festival, did a little wine tasting in Carmel Valley, and had a sing-a-long before dinner each evening.

Before I knew it the summer was almost over. Robin and Jim invited me to spend Labor Day with them at their condo in Park City, Utah. Flying again, but not quite solo. Utah is beautiful in summer. The mountains are covered with evergreens and aspen. We drove through canyons and passes to visit Sundance, and another day even higher up to a funky little restaurant called the Silver Fork. Long ago silver mining was the big industry. We had dinner one night with Will and Malia in their new little house in Salt Lake City. We ate outside in their backyard, after our sing-a-long, and it was delightful. The next afternoon Judy Wolf had a shower for Malia, who is expecting a baby in November, and that was fun too. We visited Will at Huntsman Hospital where he works as an RN. It is a beautiful facility.

Of course Robin and I did the fantastic 70% off Sale at the discount mall. It's great to shop with her as she is very honest as to whether something looks good or not.

We had dinner at the St. Regis, whose dining room is reached by riding a funicular. The martini that I ordered was so small that I asked if the bar tender was a midget. The answer was "no," but Utah state law requires that only 1.5 ounces of liquor be served per drink. Well now I know.

Aside from the fact that I was bothered by the high altitude, I really had a great time. My family is the best!

● ● ●

The Bluest Skies, the Whitest Clouds
Kiahuna, Poipu Beach, Kauai, October 2016

My daughter Robin and I have spent a week together here, and it was wonderful. Since my husband and I bought this place in 1973 when I was 42 I have been coming here for R&R, family vacations and celebrations (our 50th and 60th wedding anniversaries), and once meeting Bob and our son Bill here on their way home from climbing Mt. Everest.

It has been more than half my life. It brought back so many happy memories of Bob and good times together when we were younger. How fortunate I have been to sit on the patio at the end of the day and enjoy the gentle breeze and the beautiful view of the green lawn edged with palm trees and tropical flowers. Just beyond, the vast Pacific Ocean, waves rolling on to the beach.

I don't go in the ocean anymore due to my knee replacement, but it is enough to take in the sight of it, hear the waves crashing, and smell the air filled with the scent of flowers.

Robin and I have had Mai-Tais at sunset at the water's edge. We've made our own sashimi from fresh caught ahi and served it on plates Bob and I found at a little shop in Nigiri, the airport town that serves Tokyo.

We've driven to many of our favorite spots on the island to see what if anything is new. Thankfully, not too much, although a lot of land that used to be open is being developed for housing. We went to a craft fair and bought some wonderful handmade items.

On Saturday night we went to the Robert Louis Stevenson Library at the Hyatt Regency for martinis and sushi, and stayed for the Hawaiian music afterward. Robin and I had dressed up and wore our Niihau leis—the waitress asked if we were residents.

Robin walks and swims and snorkels everyday, and has seen some great fish.

We've both read and I have done three watercolors. Most of all, we've just relaxed. Easy for me to say, as Robin does all the work.

On Sunday morning she took me to her favorite breakfast place in Kalaheo, a wonderful locals' hangout with the freshest local produce. We drove on to Hanapepe, a town garlanded in bougainvillea of every color. We stopped at the Russian Fort (a short-lived occupation, as Kauai must have been too hot for them). Then on to Waimea and last of all Kahala, a beautiful white sand beach beyond a rusting away sugar mill, where we turned around and headed back to Kiahuna.

We invited Karen and Dean Barbieri, friends of Robin's from Piedmont, for cocktails and pupus Sunday evening. Karen has been coming to Poipu Beach since she was a child and before Kiahuna existed. Her father installed much of the irrigation for the cane fields. There were lots of stories of old Hawaii to swap. We took our drinks down to the water's edge to watch the sunset. Another perfect day.

There is nothing better than being able to spend time with a loved one in a beautiful place.

• • •

 Chapter Four

Reflections on Life

Yang Lian Island (#2)

Like a boat sailing since the day you were born

Never slowing down its disconsolate speed.

Always arriving yet, underfoot drawn away by the ebbing tide

Life goes on without stopping

Until the final adventure.

Truly Unexpected

A rumbling in the distance woke me up. Could it be thunder? Something I have rarely heard in California. I got out of bed and went to the room across the hall with an even better view out over the ocean. Dawn was breaking at about 6:00 am.

When I saw lightning I counted: one one-thousand, two one-thousand, etc. until the thunder came, helping me determine how far away the lightning was striking. My dad taught me to do this as a little girl, sitting on the front porch together, watching the storms in the sky over Brooklyn.

My grandmother, who lived with us, was very afraid of lightning, and Daddy wanted to make sure I wouldn't be; so there we'd sit, me snuggled up to him so strong and brave, and he would tell me that the angels were bowling. That's what caused the big rumbles, as their balls rolled through the heavens. Lightning, "Oh look! One of them got a strike!"

Thunderstorms were always a special time for us, and the very unexpected one on Sunday morning brought it all back.

Daddy, are you one of those angels bowling now? I'd like to think you are.

• • •

Who would you like to have a meal with?

Barack Obama   Amelia Earhartt   or Barbara Fritchey

Barbara Fritchey –

My mother named me for you because she wanted me to be brave and strong. So I'm inviting you to lunch to quiz you on how you were able to be that way.

When the Rebel soldiers came through Fredericksburg, Maryland during the Civil War, you hung out the flag and yelled to the troops going by, "Shoot if you may this old grey head, but spare your country's flag." What gave you the courage to do that? You could have been killed.

Would you like coffee or tea with your salad? I've made biscuits and we'll have strawberries for dessert.

So it was just an impulse. You were sick and tired of brother killing brother, and what had been beautiful fields of produce, littered with dead bodies. You had lived a peaceful and productive life. You had, at your age, little to lose so you took a stand, hoping it might change things.

Wars have continued to rage up until this day. I stood up in a small and safe way opposing our country's involvement in Vietnam by contributing to an anti-war ad in a newspaper, but you put your life on the line.

I admire you so much. If only there was a way we could stop brother killing brother (we <u>are</u> all brothers as members of the human race) now.

Tell me, Barbara, what do you suggest?

What I like and don't like

I like sunshine and rain. I don't like overcast.

I like real people, not phonies.

I like kids and dogs, cats not so much.

I like to be warm and cozy. I don't like feeling cold.

I like beauty: in nature, music, and art. I don't like ugliness in any of those areas.

I like ice cream, avocadoes, steak and gin martinis.

I like to sing, read and play bridge.

I like to watch PBS. I don't like to watch hockey, soap operas, or sit-coms.

I like honesty. I don't like lies.

I like kindness. I don't like meanness.

It seems that there are more things I like than don't like, and that's good!

Reading the article on author David McCullough that appeared in the *Wall Street Journal* a few weeks ago was like a walk down memory lane for me.

He is probably a few years younger, but what we did as children was very similar: dinner with the family around the dining room table every evening (no electronic devices). Conversation was our entertainment as well as communication. Everyone told what they'd done that day with comments by the others. Advice was given: "always be polite," from my mother; "stand up to bullies," from my father.

We had a great deal of freedom. We walked to school unaccompanied by parents, rode our bikes as far as we could peddle, sometimes 10-20 miles away. We were sent to the grocery store and post office on errands. We collected scrap metal for the war effort, and from the age of 12 on, we were allowed to go to New York City by bus and then subway to see a movie and stage show at Radio City Music Hall, The Roxy, or Paramount. We always had lunch at the Automat, and were able to return home safely without incident.

There were trips to museums and Broadway shows with parents, the Bronx Zoo, and the Brooklyn Botanical Gardens. New York was called the "Empire State" because it had everything and I believed that to be true until I moved to California and fell in love with another state. But I would not, to this day, swap my childhood in New York.

● ● ●

There were three very important people in my childhood that shaped my values and personality: My mother, father, and grandmother.

My mother was an only child. Her parents had divorced before she was five. Her father had been unfaithful and those

Dad and Mom.

were the grounds for their divorce in the early 1900s, a time when divorce was much less common then it is today. My mother felt it was a stigma that she carried with her through her childhood. She said she would never divorce and do that to her children.

When I married, her words were, "you've made your bed and now you will have to lie in it." So I did with a determination that it was a good decision. She had married at 17 to get away from what, at times, must have been a distressing situation at home. However, her mother either lived with us or we with her until she died. So much for escape.

My dad was orphaned as a baby and became the ward of an aunt and uncle. There was little affection and lots of work for him growing up. They met and, at 17 and 20, must have thought that together they could have a better life. When I came along, and then my brothers, it was apparent that their family was the most important thing in the world to both of them. I won't say we were spoiled, because we weren't, but we had a great sense of security that our parents and home would always be there for us. That never changed, and each of us developed those same family values. Thank you Mom and Dad.

My grandmother, who was a constant presence in our lives, seemed always to be sad, ailing, and worried. Listening to her list her complaints and ailments at the breakfast table each morning made me promise myself that when I grew up I would never be sick or sad. In a way I unconsciously decided that the only one responsible for making me happy was me. After 84 years of putting this to practice, I must say "thank you, Nana. Your negative attitude shaped my positive one."

● ● ●

Every summer I listen and look for fireflies, sunsets, farmers markets brimming with the fruits and vegetables of the season. Mostly I hear the sounds of hammers and bulldozers, remodeling, repairing, building. I see fog drifting in over the ocean. I see tourists in summer clothes on 17 Mile Drive and think they don't know Pebble Beach in summer. I do, but I still wish for an occasional hot summer day sitting outside, cooling off with a glass of ice tea or a gin and tonic. You can't have it all, so I'll be happy with the memories of hot summer days and glad for the cool Pacific Ocean just outside my door.

● ● ●

Brooklyn, NY

Happy days on shady tree-lined streets.
Only child doted on by family and neighbors.

Coney Island, NY

Wool bathing suits on Momma, and Nana and me.

Staten Island

On Sunday afternoon I attended a matinee performance of *Sweet Charity* with Margaret. In Act II Sweet Charity's boyfriend proposes to her at the top of the Parachute Jump at Coney Island. This triggered a great memory for me. In 1954, my husband Bob was working for JP Morgan on Wall Street in Manhattan. We had looked for an affordable apartment all over that borough without success when a friend mentioned looking into some townhouses on Grymes Hill on Staten Island.

These were the days before the Verrazano Bridge, but dependable ferries sailed between Manhattan landing at the foot of Wall Street as well as Brooklyn. Grymes Hill is actually the highest elevation on the Atlantic seaboard. We took an apartment there.

At the same time my doctor ordered bedrest for me until the arrival of our first child in December. I would go from the bedroom in the morning to our convertible couch in the living room where I spent the day reading, sewing and knitting. My view out our front window was the Narrows, which all the big ships passed through on their way to NY Harbor and the Parachute Jump at Coney Island. I felt very lucky. In December, our wonderful daughter Robin was born, healthy and brave enough to go upon the Parachute Jump, something I could never do.

The brave story of Inge's family escaping Russian-occupied East Germany after World War II inspired me to go back to the beginning of how all our ancestors got here. Some came by boat, small ones at that, leaving almost all they'd had behind to escape religious or political persecution. Some to have land to farm and call their own. Some came by foot, crawling through tunnels, under barriers, or forging rivers.

All of us are here because someone before us was brave enough to take a chance on a better life. No wonder our country is known as "the land of the free and the home of the brave."

I hope we will not become a country of "last one in shut the door," but continue to welcome all those who seek a better life.

● ● ●

My first encouragement (sort of)

I attended and, yes, eventually graduated from Sewanhaka High School in Floral Park, New York. It was a central high school taking in five towns and named for an American Indian chief. Every team and organization at Sewanhaka had an American Indian-related name.

I tried out for cheerleader—not coordinated enough; Pom-Pom girl—not sexy enough. I was awful at math—not smart enough. But hold on, I was an honors English student. In my junior year I was given the choice to take Journalism instead of English. Our school paper was *The Chieftain*, published twice a week. Not only was I expected to write news articles, but be able to set up, type, layout and develop headlines. I loved it.

In my senior year I was offered the chance to join the radio crew of our just-opened FM radio station WSHSFM. We even had a UPI ticker tape machine that ran continuously, and it was from this that we selected items that made up our hourly newscasts.

We also had old radio scripts from shows like "The Shadow." I got to play "Margo," The Shadow's cohort/girlfriend. At times we would run out of script material and that was referred to as "dead air," something we were determined never to have. It was then that our teacher Mr. Gregory would say, "put Barbara on. She can talk about nothing and make it sound interesting, a regular Mary Margaret McBride." Well, of course I was encouraged! That was some almost 70 years ago and I am still writing and as you may have noticed, have never stopped talking.

Holding Hands

Few things are sweeter than holding hands. My mother and I would hold hands when going shopping or going downtown, which was either Brooklyn or New York City. We swing our held hands down the street. Evidence that we were off for a good time.

My dad held my hand while I balanced myself one step at a time on top of the huge water pipes at the water works where we'd go on Sunday mornings, he in his Chesterfield coat and derby hat, me in my Sunday best outfit. I knew I would never fall off while Daddy was holding my hand.

When I met Bob, the first indication I had that he really liked me was when he took my hand and held it. We were still holding hands after almost 70 years together: at the movies, watching TV, walking. And now that I am 84, the children and grandchildren, whose hands I've held over the years, take my hand to help me get in or out of cars, up steps, and over curbs. There are few things sweeter than holding hands.

● ● ●

Today is blessed
Because you are part of it
Be happy, come with me

I've learned that the easiest way to grow as a person is to surround myself with people smarter than I am. I would also add younger and positive. I decided at a certain point to eliminate everything negative from my life. I don't have that much time left to deal with people or things who are not enjoyable.

My writing class has brought me—and continues to bring me—so much pleasure because I am learning so much from all of you. Everyone has a story, a life experience that is unique. All of them deserving of accepting and understanding. I've also learned how fortunate my life has been compared to others', and to be thankful for it.

● ● ●

"Autumn in New York" is a song that always moves me. Probably because that was where I first experienced autumn. Leaves turning orange and amber, then falling to the ground to be raked up and burned. Even recalling the smell of those fires brings pleasant memories.

The hardest part of moving to California for me was the lack of seasons, not being able to remember when things had happened by recalling snow on the ground, trees budding, hot days, leaves falling. I did get used to the year-round moderate climate, and now as an older person, I appreciate it. No leaves to rake, no snow to shovel, no hot searing days. Thank you God for making my life more simple in my old age.

But getting back to autumn in New York: the hemp rug in the living room was rolled up and put away. The wool carpet was put down. The sheer white "Priscilla" curtains were carefully washed and put on stretchers to dry. Heavy damask drapes went up in their place. On the outside of our house, screens came out and storm windows went in. House prepared, we went to the furriers and took our fur coats out of cold storage. A new theatre season opened on Broadway, and we talked about what we might want to see. School began with some new clothes and always new shoes. Football games and Sock Hops. Autumn was a fun time of new beginnings and old celebrations: Halloween and Thanksgiving. I loved autumn in New York!

● ● ●

I want to be famous for

Making you smile

Or even laugh

For always remembering

Your birthday and singing, off key, Happy Birthday to You

For listening to

And understanding

Your thoughts

And even your music

Spring

Blossoms burst on

Branches after softly

Falling rain

Life comes back anew

Sunday dinner at Uncle John's and Aunt Flossie's house in the Gravesend section of Brooklyn in the early 1930s was on the last bit of farm land owned by my father's family, who had farmed it since the 1600s. The original house had many additions that had been added as needed, making it so much more interesting to me. The three of us—Momma, Daddy and I—would drive into the yard and park near the barn, which housed a couple of old horses. I was sure to get a ride on one—Daddy leading him around by the reins while I hung on to the saddle horn. There was also a sizable pigeon coop for carrier pigeons, which were supposed to carry messages, I never knew to whom or why. We always went in the house through the kitchen. Aunt Flossie had both a gas stove and a wood stove. Both were usually going with wonderful aromas wafting from each—biscuits in the wood stove, and a big roast. Two steps up to the dining room, the largest room in the house. Big round table, where there was always room for one more. Behind the dining room door there was a large shopping bag filled with old toys hanging on the doorknob for me to play with.

Aunt Flossie and Uncle John had three grown children but no grandchildren as of yet, so that bag of toys had been put together for me. All of us were so welcome there. There was a door in the kitchen that led to the staircase, which led to a tiny room that was said to be a hiding place for slaves, a stop along the Underground Railway during the Civil War.

The shed next to the kitchen was full of stuff. My favorite things being a wicker doll carriage with a big doll in it that I wheeled around the yard, singing to it.

The living room held a piano and an organ, but the only time I ever remember it being used was for family funerals when the Dutch Reformed minister would come to the house to lead in prayers and the beloved family member would be there in a coffin until taken to the church graveyard for burial.

The basement had a dirt floor, and the supports of the house were solid tree trunks with the bark still on. The basement or cellar was filled with furniture from many bygone eras. I have two chairs that came from there, and I consider them family treasures.

All the bedrooms were upstairs under the dormered roof. Every ceiling slanted. Sunday dinner at that big round table was heaven to me. The house has been demolished, the land probably used to build apartment houses. The church, built in 1659, remains as an historic site. If only I could go back to see it one more time as it was, what a joy that would be.

● ● ●

Watermelons

Watermelons speak of summer. Have you ever been selecting one and noticed various techniques used to find just the right one? There are sniffers, shakers, and people who push against the spot on the bottom where the melon once connected to the vine. Who is to know what's best?

Lately watermelons have been produced to be seedless, but what fun it once was to sit on the porch and spit those big black seeds out on the lawn. Parents cautioning us not to swallow any pits, and if you did a watermelon would grow in your stomach.

When I was four years old my mother became pregnant. I was amazed when she brought my brother home from the hospital. I thought it would be a watermelon.

A Magical Christmas

The year was 1935, deep into the Great Depression. I was four years old. We were living on the top floor of a big old house in Brooklyn, Momma, Daddy and me. I liked it there because just downstairs there was a girl named June, my age, and we played together every day without ever going outdoors if we didn't want to.

There was lots of snow that Christmas time, and it piled up high on the roof. I had asked Santa for a Shirley Temple doll. I had seen all the Shirley Temple movies with my parents. She was my idol.

Momma told me I would have to be very good to have my wish come true, but also to remember if I heard Santa on Christmas Eve I was not to get out of bed and surprise him putting presents under the tree. That would be really bad.

I was as good as I was able to be. On Christmas Eve, I brushed my teeth, got into my pajamas and slipped into my bed under the eaves. I had not been asleep very long when I was awakened by a huge thud. Oh boy! Santa's sleigh must have landed on our roof! How I wanted to look and see, but I remembered what Momma had told me and slid further down in bed and even pulled the covers up over my head. No peeking for me!

On Christmas morning, I discovered my wish had come true. There was a beautiful Shirley Temple doll with her head of blonde curls, dimples and perfect little white teeth. She was wearing a party dress.

I was so happy, and I told Momma and Daddy that I'd heard Santa's sleigh land on the roof but had done what I was told and didn't get up. Sure was a good thing I didn't scare him away before he left Shirley Temple!

Many years later, my mother told me what she remembered

about that Christmas: our little family was just about making it. Daddy had had to give up his trucking business, as the Mafia was demanding what they called "protection money." In other words, if you didn't pay to be "protected," anything could happen to you or your property.

Dad then followed a procedure of going to what was called a Shape Up Area early every morning, and waited on line hoping to get a job for that day, usually involving manual labor, to bring home enough money to pay expenses.

He would not join the WPA and go on a government dole. He would take whatever job there was to support his family. They both wanted very much for me to have that Shirley Temple doll. So Momma went to the toy store on King's Highway and put the doll on lay-away, promising to pay 25 cents a week until it was paid for. She was able to bring the last quarter in on Christmas Eve just before the shop closed.

But what about the big thud on the roof that I was sure was Santa's sleigh landing? Oh, she said, that was snow sliding off the roof.

I still think it was the sleigh and as I always say, "Everything I learned about being a parent I learned from my parents."

● ● ●

On the recent passing of John Glenn, a true American hero, brave enough to crawl into that small space capsule and do what no American had done before: orbit the earth three times, alone.

We were living in Woodacres, Maryland, a suburb of Washington D.C. Robin was five, Bill was four and Peter was a baby. I picked up the *Washington Post* and discovered that there would be a parade downtown to welcome our brave astronaut home.

This seemed like a very historic occasion to me, so I bundled the children up, got everyone in the car, drove downtown, and found a parking spot. With Robin and Bill in either hand, and Peter strapped to my back, we headed to the parade route. Maybe because we were all short, or that I looked like I had my hands full, the crowd parted and we found ourselves right up front.

The first car to come by was the convertible with John Glenn and his wife Annie, both smiling and waving. The next convertible carried John Glenn's mother. She was smiling and waving too. And then she spotted Robin and Bill, and looking right at them, waved just to them. Being polite little people, they waved back. So in our small way, we became part of that historic day.

Robin came to visit me this weekend, and I asked her if she remembered. She did, and told me she had told her fellow workers about it. Their reaction was, of course, "Robin, you always have had an exciting life."

The next time I saw John Glenn up front and in person was the night the five of us waited on line outside the Capitol's Rotunda to view the coffin of President Kennedy and pay our respects. He walked by with Averell Harriman. Everyone so solemn and sad.

• • •

It was a mixed berry pie, black and blue berries.

I had pie for breakfast this morning. It reminded me of the days growing up in Franklin Square, in the little brick bungalow on Hoffman Street. Momma insisted that we have breakfast before leaving for school. It didn't matter to her what we ate as long as we ate something.

Dad was always the first one up at 3:00 am every morning. He usually had what was left over from last night's dinner. He worked hard as a wholesale milkman, delivering to supermarkets in New York City, hauling cases of milk and other dairy products into the stores every morning before they opened.

Momma, my brothers, and I got up around 7:00 or 8:00 to get to school by 9:00. Perusing the fridge for something that might appeal, it might be pie or cake, or even a tuna fish sandwich. If all else failed, a bowl of ice cream was always good.

When I had three children of my own, I followed the same rule. You must eat something before you leave for school, and it can be anything. My children have told me that their friends thought they had a pretty weird mother, but also that they were lucky.

Later, I went to lunch at Spanish Bay in honor of a good friend's "big" 70th birthday. Somehow during the happy babble of conversation I heard "Ponte Vedra." Ponte Vedra is a beautiful resort on the Atlantic, near Jacksonville, Florida. My mind went back forty or more years to an evening when Bob and I had stayed there. We were leaving a party, Bob in a Hawaiian shirt, me in a mumu. Bob spotted a bicycle leaning against a palm tree. He took it by the handlebars and told me to hop on the other bar. He said, "I'll drive you home," and we peddled back to our room, singing "Daisy, Daisy!"

I guessed we had stolen a bike, or at best borrowed one without permission. It was wonderful, gliding down the path to our room under the stars with the person I loved. We parked the bike outside our room. In the morning it was gone, hopefully returned to its rightful place.

• • •

Ode to My Mug

My mug sits quietly right next to my perky coffee maker.

It is the first thing I see in the morning and the last at night.

It warms my hands when filled with coffee and my heart when
 I read the message on its side.

A gift from my daughter.

It tells me all day long, "I love you Mom."

It's Christmastime. I've given a lot of thought to and actually bought many gifts for family and friends, but I just can't seem to put up a lot of decorations. Everything dragged out of that huge closet under the staircase eventually will have to go back in again. And it all seems to take more energy than I have to spare.

Outside Lucky's grocery store they have miniature real pine trees that actually smell like pine and are probably the tops of Noble Firs. I bought one and put it on the side of the fireplace hearth in my family room, adjacent to the kitchen, where I spend most of my time. I tied a red ribbon on top and strung a string of 100 tiny white lights around it. Then I retired the fading white orchid on the coffee table and replaced it with a red poinsettia from Rite Aid.

It is a much scaled down Christmas display, but it seems just right for me this year.

Rose petals blow

Across the lawn, wind is strong

Whipping through tree canopies

Taking away the patio umbrella

Stronger than my arms to hold on.

Mother nature is cleaning house.

I recently had an accident. On my way to class last week, when I stopped to pick up my eggs on Casanova St., instead of putting my car in park, I only got as far as neutral. Result: car rolled down the street, knocked out a stop sign, and rolled on, to be stopped by an ancient pine tree.

Thank goodness no one was hurt. My car sustained some damage, all cosmetic. The tree is fine, as am I, not having been in the car that did this all on its own! This incident reminded me of another accident.

● ● ●

Another Accident Long Ago

My dad drove a large refrigerated cab-over-engine White truck, White being the manufacturer's name, on his wholesale milk route delivering to supermarkets in New York City.

Early in the morning on a St. Patrick's Day, a day more grandly celebrated in New York and Chicago than Dublin, the big White was parked at a juncture facing O'Leary's Bar.

While Dad was unloading his milk order to the A&P across the way, the truck slowly rolled into O'Leary's Bar on the most profitable day of the year for any Irish bar. Of course, my dad was upset. He'd had a perfect driving record, and of course he felt bad for O'Leary.

Fortunately he'd left a note in the cab of the truck the day before, at the end of work, saying, "check brakes" for the mechanics.

He received the Safe Driving Award that year, much to the amusement of the other drivers, one of whom had drawn a cartoon of Cropsey's truck half way into O'Leary's Bar on St. Patrick's Day. It hung in my dad's garage.

Do you think this sort of accident can be hereditary?

● ● ●

My Session With the Judge

After receiving a notice to appear at the DMV for an interview with a judge following the incident of my car rolling down Casanova St. and into a tree, I arrived early and prepared. I had studied the driver's manual and attended the week before a "Safe Driving for Seniors" workshop, from which I received a certificate of participation. I brought that along as well as the list of medications I take daily, and dosages.

Per instructions I knocked on the door of the judge's office. He welcomed me in and invited me to sit down. He then explained that he would ask me a series of set questions and this would all be recorded with my permission, which I gave.

He said he would speak softly as the room was not soundproofed. He began by asking me how long I had been driving. Answer: 65 years. Then he described the path of my car down the street, and objects it had hit, including a stop sign. Was that correct? My answer: I did not witness any of that." I saw my car resting against a tree and acknowledged that the fault was mine for failing to apply the parking brake.

The judge said the Carmel police officer found me upset. My reply, "Yes, of course I was." The officer offered to accompany me home, but I told him I would go on to my class at the Foundation and then call my insurance agent.

After doing that, at the insurance agent's instruction, I visited two body shops for estimates to repair the damage and, on my own, also went to the Marlow Mercedes Works to see if the inner workings of the car were in good shape.

The answer to that was positive, so I decided to have the cosmetic repairs to the body done and keep my car. It had been a gift from husband on our 50th wedding anniversary. Toward the end of his life when he had macular degeneration and I became his driver, he bought me a chauffeur's cap, and he sat in the back seat.

The judge asked if I was prepared to take the written test today. I answered, "Yes."

He said, "When did you last study the driver's manual?"

And my answer, "Yesterday."

He turned off the recorder and said to me, "We're not supposed to express any religious feelings, but I do feel that we will be reunited with our loved ones." I agreed. He said he would make a determination in 5-10 days as to my need for reexamination. I wait to hear from him.

The judge was very kind and I discovered that I was very relaxed during the interview. In a way, that was a revelation.

A slow infusion of light

Enters the room

Night has passed

Another day begins

What will it bring

Good things I hope

News from friends

A flower opening in the garden

A bird's song just outside

Best of all ... rain

September 15, 2015

The House I Live In

I've lived in many nice homes including the ones I grew up in, and too often dream of walking through them and seeing people who lived there, but the one I live in now is the one I've lived in longest, and with my husband, designed.

While visiting friends on Cormorant Road in the 80s, they suggested that we buy a house in Pebble Beach, ten years before retiring, as real estate in the area was going up at a rapid rate.

Whenever a house on their block would go on the market, Bob or I would fly out from Chicago to check it out. On one such trip to see one of these houses, a Realtor standing at the front door of a newly for sale property waved to us to come in.

It was on the wrong side of the street, but as we held open the door and looked back, we had a clear view of the ocean. The house was centered directly across from an easement to the Monterey Peninsula Country Club golf course.

The house we were taken to see held no appeal to us, but the little house straddling the easement did and was so much more affordable. Bob said what we would do was hire an architect who would be willing to work with our son Bill who would build it. We closed the deal and started planning our dream house. Our only constraint was that we had to follow the original footprint.

We decided to go up a story, have a large living room, dining room, kitchen, family room library, small bedroom and bath along with laundry room on the first floor. Second floor would have master bedroom with separate dressing rooms at either side of a bathroom containing a Jacuzzi tub big enough for two, a walk-in shower, and a toilet. A guest bedroom with full bath and an upstairs study/media room with a hide-a-bed sofa for more guest space when needed.

Bob and I spent many hours at the Lake Forest library studying copies of *Architectural Digest* for ideas, and we got a few. We decided to honor our East Coast roots by having a cedar shingle exterior with white trim.

I wanted an English garden spilling over with flowers. Our Japanese landscaper didn't quite get it, but he came close and as the years have gone by it's a compromise between English and California favorites.

After two years of construction our house was completed. Whenever we could come out for a week or two, we would help. I got to nail on some of the shingles and paint the moldings before they were installed. Bob carried the plaster up to the roof to finish the chimneys.

We rented the house until Bob retired. Our renters were extremely considerate and it was still like new when we moved in, in 1992. I was 61 and Bob was 63.

We always hosted Thanksgiving and Christmas here, as well as special occasions like birthdays and Robin and Jim's wedding. Friends came every year for the AT&T. Our grandsons came every summer for Camp Moody. This house is crammed with happy memories.

On my 80th birthday, five years ago, I asked for a plaque to go over our garden gate entrance. It says "Contentment" and that is how we have always felt here. Now that I have been alone here for two years, I still feel content in a home filled with love and joy.

● ● ●

Forgiveness

To carry a grudge is to be unforgiving,
  which is to be burdened.
Lighten your load ... forgive.

Over the years I have forgiven so many things both small and large. One of the things I discovered was that in the case of things I was denied, when I was able to have them, I no longer wanted them. They really didn't matter. What burden it would have been to carry a grudge, to disturb a relationship, only to discover what I wanted but didn't get wasn't that important.

Forgiveness is a gift you give yourself and will always make you a better person. As for insults and hurt feelings, when a person cannot say "sorry," they sometimes make up to you in other ways that may even be more meaningful.

Forgive, and if you are able, forget about it.

My Garden

I've had many gardens over the years. The first one was as a little girl in the back yard of our house in Franklin Square. My mother always planted tomatoes. The seeds she always gave me to plant were radishes. One year, I asked her why I always got radishes. Her reply was that no matter what, they would always grow. I would have a successful crop and feel proud of myself. And, of course, my dad loved radishes! He would dip them in salt and eat them whole. Mom sliced them and put them in our nightly salads.

At our first house after Bob and I were married and now had two children, and another on the way, we planted a vegetable garden: tomatoes of course, and way back then, kale and a row of corn and zucchini. Robin and Bill loved to harvest what we would include in our dinner each night. But I wanted more. We planted

Blaze red rambling roses to climb on and conceal the fence I considered ugly. Then I got my hands on a *Jackson and Perkins* catalogue and ordered tea roses in a variety of colors and larkspur in shades of blue to back them up. My order arrived during the ninth month of my pregnancy with Peter, baby number three. I asked Bob to plant the new arrivals. He said, sure, but not right now. It was June 11, baby due on July 4. I couldn't wait, got out a spade and dug up the ground along the back fence, and on completion of the task, promptly went into labor that lasted off and on for four days. Peter was born June 16. The garden was beautiful by the way.

At the house in Woodacres, Bob and I planted rhododendrons. In Lake Forest it was always impatiens every spring, several flats all over in every color to celebrate the end of the long Illinois winter, and a bed of peonies that bloomed on our anniversary every year.

Looking over my garden in Los Altos Hills, at the time our house was for sale as we were moving to Lake Forest, Illinois, the roses looked fine as did the eggplant in the same bed. Then my eye caught a plant or rather a number of plants not planted by me. The leaf looked familiar. I'd seen it on posters and even T-shirts. Of course it was marijuana. I promptly pulled it up and destroyed it.

When my teenage son and his best buddy Chris came home from school, I quizzed them about my discovery. They were devastated that it had been destroyed, as according to them it was worth a lot of money and they were planning to sell it. I countered with the fact that realtors and prospective buyers were in and out of our garden every day, and if the marijuana had been discovered we all could have been in big trouble.

Now, my 60-year old son Bill grows his own pot in his garden on Lopez Island, Washington, where it is now legal.

Twenty-five years ago I planted my current garden, making sure to include hydrangea, roses, lilies, geraniums, agapanthus, bird of paradise and protea. When the drought years came, I put more and more succulents in. As a member of Ikibana, I put a flower arrangement in the Tokomomo at Westland House every month. The flowers are always from my garden. It is a labor of love. Nothing gives me greater satisfaction.

Thomas Jefferson said that everyone should have a garden to be close to the soil, the basics of life. I believe that too. Come into my garden, it's through the gate with the Contentment sign above it, and on a sunny day you will find me on the deck, enjoying the fresh air and the flowers.

● ● ●

I rest in the grace of the world and am free.

To be living in such a beautiful place is to feel a special grace, a privilege, a blessing. Through one window, the ocean; another, my garden. Do I deserve all this? Probably not, but I do appreciated it and I thank the powers that be for letting me experience all this beauty and peace in my lifetime. If there is a heaven I hope to go there, but if there isn't, I have had it here on earth.

● ● ●

> **"My mission in life is not merely to survive,
> but to thrive; and to do so with some passion,
> some compassion, some humor, and some style."**
>
> *– Maya Angelou*

As a little girl my dad would take me to the carousel at Coney Island. He always encouraged me to reach for the brass ring even though my arm wasn't long enough to reach it. Of course one day it was. What a thrill to get it at last. Sometimes the trying, the chase, is even better than at last achieving the goal.

To live life with passion and compassion makes it worth living, but it's essential to have a sense of humor, especially in regard to oneself at times when things don't always work out as planned. At times like this it's even more important to look good even when failing. You only go around once, do it with passion, compassion humor and style!

We were asked to choose a favorite letter of the alphabet. Well I can't because I like them all. Combined they make words and words strung together can make lists, letters, stories, books.

As an example I will tell you a story of what last week was like for me: On Monday, my grandson Will and his wife Malia arrived at my house with my first great grandchild, Maisie. Maisie's name was inspired by a series of books her mom read while pregnant, about "Maisie Dobbs," detective, psychiatrist.

Maisie Sanford is seven months old. She sits up, smiles, laughs, has chubby pink cheeks, big blue eyes, is happy all the time, and I am crazy about her. We spent the next three days playing with her and watching her grow and learn new things everyday.

On Wednesday evening, my brother Jeff arrived from Florida. He could also be known as the crazy uncle, as he is also a happy, full of fun person. Are you noticing certain family traits here?

After we saw the Sanford family off on Thursday morning, Jeff and I went to the Talbott's Warehouse sale. Yes, he likes to shop too, just like his big sister. That evening Jeff took me out to dinner on what would have been my 65th anniversary. I chose one of Bob's favorite restaurants, China Delight. After we were seated Jeff said he would like to interview me about the story of how I met my husband and our life together. He said, "I know it's in your book, but I'd like to hear you tell it." It was wonderful recalling so many happy years.

On Friday Jeff and I drove to my daughter Robin's home in Berkeley. We all went shopping as Robin is redecorating. Here come those genes again!

On Saturday Robin, Jeff and I drove to Napa to visit my son Peter and wife Mara who were having a garden party. Saw lots of old friends, drove back to Berkeley in time for supper, which we ate on the deck overlooking San Francisco Bay, and watched the planes taking off from the airport on a beautiful star-lit night.

After breakfast on Sunday Jeff and I drove back to Pebble Beach. Jeff spotted the collage I had made at Illia's workshop and asked if he might have it. I was flattered, so of course said yes. The next morning we took it to UPS to have it shipped to Florida and its new home. Then drove Jeff to the Airbus station in Monterey. What a busy wonderful week seeing so many family members and having so much fun. I must admit I was pooped, but wouldn't change a thing. I believe in telling this story that I used all the letters of the alphabet. I love them all.

● ● ●

The Things They Left Behind

Bob's grandmother had tatted lace edging on pillowcases for us when we married. When the percale fabric wore out, I cut off the lace and incorporated on to a decoupage waste basket I made for our daughter's bedroom. She still has it.

When my mother passed away, my brother, sister-in-law and I sorted through her things, deciding what to keep and what to donate to charitable causes. My mom had been an accomplished seamstress and one of the things I chose to keep was a jar of odd buttons. It's amazing how many times I find just the perfect button in that jar to replace one that's been lost. I always say, "Thank you, Momma."

Daddy made me a recipe holder from a clothespin mounted on a block of wood. It's great to think of him when I'm cooking.

Bob in one of his cashmere sweaters that I wear now.

Bob left many wonderful things, but I think I feel closest to him when I'm wearing one of his cashmere sweaters.

How interesting, the connections we make with the things they left behind, and the memory of their love.

I am a party animal! I love to go to and to give parties. Here are a few my husband and I have given over the years:

New Year's Eve in Woodacres, Maryland. We cleared the furniture out of the dining room. Bob made a dance floor out of plywood. We sprinkled it with dance floor wax and had our neighbors in to celebrate New Year's. The next day Bob sawed up the plywood and made a storage unit for the children's toys.

A Hawaiian party in Lake Forest, Illinois. We invited everyone in the area who had ever rented our condo in Kauai. We had a combo playing Hawaiian music, and served Mai Tais and pupus. As we toasted, we observed that one thing we all had in common was that at one time we had each slept in the same bed.

My 50th birthday. Bob hired the same combo on the condition that they would let me sing with the band. This was a surprise for me too, and first we had to find a song we all knew. It turned out to be "I'm gonna sit right down and write myself a letter." What a kick that was for me!

Murder Mystery party for Bob's office in Lake Forest. No script, just an assignment of roles. At the end of the party the murderer was revealed. Me! Bob said he knew it would be me, as my character was the wife of the victim who had been unfaithful, and he said he knew if he had ever been I would have killed him.

An unexpected party in Pebble Beach. We had been without power for going on three days. Bob had taken our grandsons on a ski trip. I thought of all the good things in the freezer soon to spoil, called up my favorite neighbors and invited them to a party that night. They brought things from their freezer too, and it turned out to be a feast. The house was lit with candles. After cocktails we sat down at the dining room and with a little thump, all the lights came on. Bob returned a few days later and said, "I hear you've had a power outage. I guess you had to throw out a lot of food."

"Oh no," I replied. "I had a party."

Listening

Especially at night I can hear the waves breaking on the shore and the seals barking. I love the sounds of the ocean. On Kauai the wind blowing through the palm trees makes a sound similar to rain on the roof, another comforting sound. On that same island roosters crowing at dawn announce the start of another day.

Here in Pebble Beach mourning doves and crows fill that role. Wind chimes tinkling tell of rising winds. So much information comes through listening.

Once I became a mother I slept with one ear open listening for sounds that a child might need me and later of an ill husband in need of help.

My hearing is good and I listen well. I prefer to talk to members of my family by phone rather than emailing as I can tell by the sounds of their voices how they are feeling. We all phone a lot, and we all listen well.

I listen intently to the stories in my writing class and so appreciate them listening to mine. It is what makes that time on Mondays so special. By listening I hear the pain, loneliness, love, sorrow and joy without interruption or commercials. Listening and seeing, two of the greatest gifts.

● ● ●

The Grapes of Wrath is one of the most unforgettable books I've ever read. The last time I remember reading it was when my son Bill was in junior high school in Palo Alto. His best friend Chris was living with us at the time after his mother's suicide. They were in the same class and assigned *The Grapes of Wrath* to read. As was my custom, I read each book any of my children were reading, so that we could discuss them together.

Quite apart from our reading of *Grapes of Wrath*, the boys asked me what my definition of a lady was. I thought for a minute and then said, "It has nothing to do with social standing. It's a quality of putting others first, as in *The Grapes of Wrath*, Ma Judd is cradling the body of her dead father in her lap. The family comes to the California border. She does not give in to her grief until they are safely on the other side, and then lets it be known that he has died. In doing so she has protected the whole family. That's my definition of a lady."

Fire

Bob and I had just ended a day of digging in our backyard. It was during the Cuban missile crisis. We were living in a suburb of Washington D.C. and felt the need for a bomb shelter, especially for our three children.

Sweaty and dirty, I retreated to our bedroom on the second floor of our brick colonial house. We had just installed a window air conditioner and Bob had bought a cheap extension cord, on sale of course.

I turned on the A.C. and stripped off the dirty clothes, throwing them on the floor. In the shower I opened a new bottle of shampoo and, starting at the top, I washed from head to toe. The shampoo, I decided, smelled like burning rubber. I'll never buy that brand again.

Feeling clean again, I toweled off and opened the door to the bedroom—to be greeted by flames. I shouted for Bob to come quick!

He bounded up the stairs grabbed my flaming padded bra by a strap and ran downstairs again to throw it on the ground and hose it down with the garden hose. Why didn't we just throw it in the shower? Oh well, second thoughts.

Meanwhile, I tamped out the rest of the fire with my wet towel. My sewing cabinet and one of the rockers on our rocking chair were lost.

Two lessons learned: never buy cheap electrical equipment (the extension cord was the cause of the fire); and forget about padded bras.

● ● ●

Change

There have been many changes in my life. The first big change was getting married at 20. There was no "trying it out" beforehand. No co-habitation. I went from my parents' house to my husband's house. Only it wasn't a house but at first a series of apartments outside army bases. I tried to make each one a home and then we'd move again.

Out of the army we moved to the campus of Indiana University in Bloomington so Bob could complete law school. Dr. Kinsey was writing his book and doing his studies on sex. On interviewing some of us law school wives we didn't understand half of the terminology of his questions. What a change that people talked about such things.

Law school finished, we returned to New York, had our first child, now that was a change! Months later, we were expecting our second child, and moved again. This time to the suburbs of Detroit where Bob took a job as a tax attorney for the Chrysler Corporation.

The style of their cars that year was called "The Forward Look" and I definitely had it. Found a doctor, a church, joined a bridge group, bought our first house. Bob went back to school at night to get a Master of Law degree at Wayne State University.

Five years later he was offered a job with the government in Washington D.C. By now we had three kids and a van full of mid-century Danish modern furniture.

We found a brick colonial house in Wood Acres, Maryland. Slowly our décor went from mid-century to antique, by way of country auctions and refinishing in our garage.

It was a short commute for Bob to the Capitol where he was on the staff of the joint committee, Senate Finance and House Ways and Means. They were writing a new tax bill.

Kennedy was president. There were balls, fireworks on the mall. It was a glamorous world. Then the tax bill passed. Kennedy was assassinated. We stood in line with the mourners to go through the rotunda.

Johnson was president. The glamour had faded. What a change. The Secretary of Treasury Henry Fowler invited Bob to be one of his special assistants. Cultural evenings at the White House with Lady Bird. Very nice!

Secretary Fowler's good friend, Jack Pope, president of FMC Corp. in San Jose, California, needs a tax attorney. Fowler recommends Bob, and we are off to California and a home in Los Altos Hills with a swimming pool. Another change.

I always thought of each relocation as a sort of resurrection. It gave me a chance to try new things. I joined a tennis team. I learned to ride a horse, became a member of the League of Women Voters and wrote a newspaper column. Except for having to clean the pool everyday, life was good; and with two teenagers and one preteen, very busy. After seven delightful years in sunny California, FMC got a new president and decided to move us all to Chicago. Oh what a change!

We went kicking and screaming to a 100-year old Victorian in Lake Forest. Restoring old house, shoveling snow, making new friends, tennis, cross-country skiing, biking, bridge, writing another newspaper column. As children go off to college, traveling with Bob on his business trips: Europe, South America, Caribbean.

Nineteen years later, retirement to Pebble Beach, California. Building our house with son Bill as our contractor. Golf, tennis, walks along the ocean, more travel. And then increasing numbers of doctor visits for Bob, 16 years worth, not a good change.

The last big change, becoming a widow and having to reinvent my life once again. This time without my partner of 63 years. Taking my daughter's advice, I plan an activity for each day to connect with people. Weekends are the hardest, but on Monday I have my writing class; Tuesday, bridge; Wednesday, lunch with an old friend; Thursday, bridge; Friday, bridge. I'm so glad I learned to play cards. Having had to give up sports, my brain is all I have left to connect with people.

● ● ●

An Unexpected Event at the Event

It happened at the Monterey Marriott Hotel, at the annual luncheon and hat fashion show put on by C.P.Y. (Community Partnership for Youth). The luncheon helps fund their programs for children at risk on the Monterey Peninsula. It is a year-round facility where kids can go after school for help with homework, sports, art and music lessons. Not only is it a worthwhile cause but also a lot of fun.

Most people who attend wear hats that are a bit over the top in more ways than one, and coordinating outfits. For example, one woman from Seaside decorated a white broad brimmed hat with little plastic cars all around to celebrate the most exciting event in Seaside in many years, the opening of In 'n' Out Burger.

There are prizes for most beautiful, creative, best coordinated, etc. As the winners in each category were chosen, they came to the stage, took a bow, then walked the runway with all the wiggle and style they could muster to celebrate the occasion.

The last one up was Renee. She wore a vintage white St. John's knit dress, white high heels, and a gorgeous white cartwheel hat. She did her thing on the stage, then down the runway and back, which had us all laughing and clapping to the band playing "New York, New York."

As she returned to the stage, she turned to face the audience and fell over. First aid was immediately provided. The bodice of the vintage dress was cut open to facilitate C.P.R. She was taken to the hospital by ambulance. She died a few hours later, but what a way to go: smiling and strutting to the applause of friends.

I hope my final exit will be that joyful.

.

Cars

I guess you always love your first car. Ours was a Tucson tan Ford convertible with red leather seats. We drove away together on our honeymoon in June 1951. A few years later we left it in Uncle Bill's garage while enjoying a weekend at Hampton Bays. Unbeknownst to us, there was a cat in the rafters who, in its frustration of not being able to get out, tore up the roof of our beautiful little car. We returned to find it in shreds. Our insurance agent, an old family friend, declared it an "Act of God," which we were covered for. And so the roof was replaced.

Further down the road, so to speak, we had another second-hand car: a red and white Plymouth station wagon to accommodate our family of three children. It had been used by the Chrysler Corporation to film its commercials with a camera mounted on its roof. Sans camera, I was driving a carpool of little girls to their weekly lesson at the Washington School of Ballet when one of the girls said, "I love your car, Mrs. Moody. You can see the road going by underneath." Sure enough, the floorboards had rusted out.

I took it to be repaired. The bill was quite reasonable, as they had soldered together a series of outdated license plates from a number of different states to cover the hole. Just when I thought everything was fixed, I went to the driveway to start it one Saturday morning, and it burst into flames. Somebody called the Bethesda Fire Department.

They arrived with a hook and ladder as well as a boat. We were a couple of miles from the Potomac, but it was a bit of overkill. All the neighbors had gathered to check out the excitement in our otherwise quiet neighborhood. I went in the house to get one of Bob's baseball hats to pass around, saying, "Looks like we'll need a new car."

We ordered our first Mercedes many years later. The children were all grown and I was self-employed as a substitute dental hygienist in the suburbs of Chicago, driving to different towns each time. Bob's idea was that he'd put the car in my name and charge it as a business expense. However the IRS did not see it his way, but it sure was fun going to Stuttgart to pick up that car, as it rolled off the assembly line, and hearing the man in the blue smock say, "Frau Moody, your car is ready." We drove it for 20 years then gave it to our son Peter who drove it for another 10.

So you can see that when my current Mercedes, at a mere 14 years, rolled down the street and into the tree, I refused to give it up as salvage, and will have it repaired, and hopefully will happily drive it for another five years, or maybe even more.

We loved all our cars and kept each one as long as the wheels rolled around and they got us where we needed to go.

The Happiest Day, January 24, 1956

Do we ever know the happiest day at the time it is happening?

On one occasion, I did. It was the day my son Bill was born, a cold January morning in the suburbs of Detroit. My husband was on a business trip to Dayton, Ohio. Our one-year-old daughter was asleep in her crib.

When it became evident that I would have to go to the hospital, I phoned Bob's friend from work who had offered to take me to the hospital in Bob's absence, then my neighbor to ask her to check on Robin when she would wake in probably two hours, and Bob to tell him where I'd be. He asked me to wait until he could get there. Obviously, he'd never had a baby.

It seemed like such a long wait for Jim to arrive, as my contractions became more frequent, then the doorbell rang and it was his beautiful wife Jane, and I knew why. She had taken the time to dress as if for church, and applied full makeup. I just grabbed my little bag and got in the car, which was running, with Jim behind the wheel. Jane was equipped with a fresh white handkerchief to wave out the window in case we had to go through any red lights. We didn't.

Jim pulled up at the main entrance of the William Beaumont Hospital in Royal Oak, Michigan and I went inside to the front desk where I was asked to present proof of my financial responsibility. Then I was taken to a labor room. On examination the doctor said, "You should have gone directly to emergency. This baby is coming fast." And he was. With a nurse propping me up by the shoulders I was able to see him emerge, a beautiful, healthy 8-pounds, 9-ounces boy, my Bill!

I was so happy that I laughed and cried all at the same time. I was euphoric! Truly one of, if not THE happiest days of my life.

.

I wanted to take art classes in high school. My parents' advice, "take something practical. You don't want to be a starving artist." So I signed up for college entrance courses. I did write, though, stories, poems, even plays in high school and college, just for the fun and joy of it. Now I think of that as a form of art. I made my own and my children's clothes, knitted and did needlepoint without using patterns. All of these forms of self-expression.

When we moved to Pebble Beach 25 years ago, I would see people on 17-Mile Drive with their easels and paints and yes that is really what I wanted to do! My walking buddy, Mary McNamara had the same ambition and one day she saw a notice in the paper about a watercolor class at the Carmel Foundation. It was free if you joined the Foundation, dues $15 a year. We signed up and began classes in Plein Aire painting with Nancy Johnson. We loved it!

We went on to acrylics with Jon Wats, oils with visiting artists at Monterey Museum, and drawing at M.P.C. Last year we went to Italy together to enjoy the marvelous art of Florence and Siena.

Yes we have done it all these years, not for money or fame, but to experience becoming, to find out what's inside of us, to make our souls grow, and for the pure joy and fun of it!

My paintings hang in homes from coast to coast in the U.S.A. and in several countries in Europe, all gifts to my family and friends. It was fun for me to gift them, and a joy to hear from the recipients that they think of me each day when they look at them.

● ● ●

A few years ago on a trip to Filoli in the springtime with friends, I was so impressed by all the beautiful spring blooms, tulips in every color, camellias, dogwood, azaleas, and then at the end of a garden path, we came upon a field of daffodils. Without even thinking, I said, "a host of golden daffodils." My friend said, "What?"

I replied, "it's from a poem by Wadsworth. It's in a book of poems Bob gave me before we were married."

When I got home I phoned her and read the poem. She said, "This is the most romantic thing I've ever heard."

P.S. She's been married 3 times.

• • •

What I Need

I need friends

I need projects

I need a book to read when I can't sleep

I need a reason to get up in the morning

I have a wonderful family

A comfortable home

A beautiful garden

An old car that runs

What more do I need?

Ray Bradbury—Read both trash and treasure

I've often said, "If I don't have something to read I'll read the labels on bottles." I read constantly; four newspapers a week—*Monterey Herald*, mostly for the obits and crossword puzzles, but I do think it is improving in news coverage; *The Wall Street Journal*, I started out as just a browser but as my husband's eyesight began to fail I would more and more read articles of interest to him as we sat together in the library after breakfast.

After Bob passed away, a little over a year ago, I continued my subscription because it makes me feel better informed on any number of subjects. *The Pine Cone* every Friday for the really local happenings; and my treat of the week, the *Sunday New York Times*.

I was so glad to see "Spotlight" win the best picture award this year, as it focused on the importance of true journalism. For the most part, the news we get on TV or radio is just a snippet of a story that we are able to explore in depth in a newspaper. It saddens me that so many great papers have had to fold over the past few years. Let's keep reading. I know I will.

My daughter and I read books together, and then discuss them, as do several of my friends. One friend and I have been exchanging books for the last 20 years. She prefers books about World War II, and I feel now that we have explored every aspect of it.

My grandchildren quiz me on what I am reading, and make lists to read. I am flattered.

On reading the travel sections in the newspaper I am always reminded of trips my husband and I have taken. Just last week there was one about Furnace Creek in Death Valley. Sure we stayed there and drove all around Death Valley. It was not a trip I would have chosen, and there were several others as well, but almost always there was something surprising to admire that made the trips worthwhile. In Death Valley it was the colors of the sand that changed during the day as the sun traveled through the sky. At night it was the unparalleled beauty of the stars with no other light to compete with them.

Maybe going along on the less glamorous trips as well as the truly wonderful ones was a factor that made our marriage a long and good one.

● ● ●

Celebrating Phyllis

My dear friend had gone to Maryland to help out her 99-year-old mother who had a stroke. Two weeks after being there, abdominal pains forced her to go to the hospital. X-rays revealed stage 4 cancer of the liver and pancreas. She texted her closest friends with this news, which was devastating to all of us.

I phoned Phyllis immediately to offer help of any kind since I was one of the few of us, being a widow, who could at a moment's notice do just about anything. Phyllis had not long ago had her 70th birthday, a mere kid in my book. Six weeks ago her husband had retired as a psychiatrist at Salinas Valley Memorial Hospital. They had made plans together for a number of trips as well as fun things to explore at home. Sometimes life doesn't seem fair.

Our group decided we would have a "Celebrate Phyllis Day" on Friday. Each person brought something from champagne to chocolate cake. There were flowers everywhere and butterfly headpieces to keep the feeling light. Each of us had written a note to let Phyllis know how special she is. They were all put in a flower-covered box for her to take home. We took a lot of pictures, made a lot of toasts. Three bottles of champagne magically disappeared.

After we settled down at the dining room table, Phyllis tapped her glass for attention and said "Ladies, I want to tell you something." This is the story she told:

○ ○ ○

In the 1960s I was teaching at Walt Whitman High School in Bethesda, Maryland. The students were primarily children of congressmen, senators, members of the diplomatic corps, etc. For reasons unknown there were a number of suicides, car accidents, and even deaths when students following online directions tried to make a bomb and blew themselves and a part of their house up.

The principal chose 12 teachers to investigate what happens after death. We visited a morgue, mortuary, cemetery and crematorium. For some reason it made me less fearful of death. So I would like you to treat me as you always have. Call at any time. Invite me to anything fun that you're doing. Let's play bridge. As long as I feel up to it I want to make the most of each day. And you can all help me. I've always felt that this group is very spiritually connected in caring for each other.

○ ○ ○

There were some tears and a lot of hugs. Phyllis with all her strength and courage had made us feel more relaxed about this horrible situation. What a classy lady!

I read the notes written by the ladies at the luncheon. My intention was to read a line from each one, but I found that the same threads ran through each one: what a special friend

Eleven of Phyllis's best friends.

Phyllis was, and how much she was loved. We all hope that our life will have made a difference. Phyllis's did. She raised the bar in kindness and consideration, making each of us better people. Thank you and God bless you, Phyllis.

Some Enchanted Evening

It was truly an enchanted evening for me. The night of my 85th birthday. It was also Valentine's Day. Love was in the air!

Before the day, I was hesitant. How would this group blend or just get along? Would they all be just too much trouble to handle? Their dietary needs—just to name one. Need to be entertained, etc.

I was so wrong. I needn't have worried about a thing. They were all considerate as can be, not only of me, but of each other.

One of the young men arrived with a cold. His two sisters insisted he take the bedroom that could have been theirs, so he could get more sleep. They slept on couches in the living room.

They entertained themselves with walks to the ocean to see the giant waves breaking over the rocks, and taking pictures of them, and the sea gulls and all of us. A trip to the Discovery Shop was also part of the entertainment, and everyone found something unique. We also discussed books and made lists of those to read.

Because all the children and grandchildren were in different locations, this occasion was the first in a long time that all of us had been together, and it was obvious everyone was enjoying catching up. It was a joy to watch.

Now it was time for the party. We piled into three cars and headed for Fandango's. Robin had reserved the wine cellar for our group of 13.

After cocktails, and before dinner, Robin led the group in, saying something nice about Babs, then everyone else joined in: She's cheerful, optimistic, an artist, writer, flower arranger. It really touched me. I looked around the room at all the people I love and told each one, briefly, why they are special to me. There was definitely a warm vibe in the room. The food was good, the wine and, of course, the company.

Then it's time to leave. Back at my house there was a wonderful cake with 85 candles accompanied by toasts, hugs and kisses, lots of laughter, more wonderful conversation. There could not have been a more enchanted evening.

● ● ●

Reminisce Magazine

I stuck my fingers in the middle of the pile of *Reminisce Magazines* that Illia had brought to the class for prompts. Without looking I brought one up to face level and there I was in the first car we ever owned—a Tucson tan Ford Convertible with red leather seats.

I was back in the '50s with an adorable little blonde-haired daughter in the back seat, along with her dark-haired little brother Bill. No seat belts or child seats. Who needed them? I even had a checked gingham dress back then, only mine was pink instead of blue.

Before we were married, Bob and I opened a joint bank account, each putting money for what we might need after that happy event.

About three weeks before our wedding, Bob's Uncle Bill

heard from a friend about a Ford convertible in excellent shape, low mileage, etc. that was for sale for $600.

Bob was in Basic Training in the army. The Korean War was on and he had been drafted. He could have gone to Officer's Training but he chose regular army as he thought he could get out sooner.

The thing was that I was left on my own to make the decision on buying the car. My parents said they would lend us the $300 lacking if I liked the car.

Uncle Bill drove me to Riverside Drive in Manhattan where the owners lived, to see it. The owners were two men, perfectly charming, living in a beautiful, immaculate apartment. The car was like that too. They garaged it nearby only using it on weekends for drives up the Hudson. With the recent advent of rental cars they'd decided renting was more economical than owning.

Of course it was love at first sight as far as I was concerned. We must have brought along Uncle Bill's friend who drove it back to Long Island, because I hadn't learned to drive yet.

The following week Bob's brother Don started my driving lessons, and in a short time I was ready for the test for my license, which arrived in the mail minutes before we left for the church for the wedding. I didn't know which I was more excited about.

My parents asked if we would like a fancy reception or the forgiveness of the car loan. We opted for the latter.

After the wedding and home reception, we loaded the car with three cardboard boxes—everything we owned—and took turns driving back to Fort Bragg, North Carolina, with a few stops at resorts along the way. That was our honeymoon, driving in our dream car with the top down. It was heaven!

● ● ●

*Recall whom you have touched
on your way through life*

    This is the second time this week I've read this sentence in two different places. The first in *The Buddha* by Deepak Chopra, and then in Ilia's prompt.

    Throughout my life I have been fortunate in having, I guess you could say, a positive attitude. A smile comes easily as well as a kind word. I don't have to think about it. It's just the way it is.

    As a child my teachers told me this; as an adult people have told me that seeing me has made their day happier.

    My children and grandchildren have all told me they have always felt unconditional love, as have my parents and brothers.

    Perhaps all of us, as we grow older and know life cannot go on forever, wonder if we have done anything to make the world a better place. I've certainly not discovered a cure for a disease, invented a marvelous invention, or brought about world peace, so I am left to hope that the smiles, kind words and unconditional love will count for something. It was all I had to give.

What Am I?

From Herbie, I am extroverted. Even a clown at times, but kind.

From Inez, polite, proper, skilled at all the household arts: cooking, sewing, making do with whatever is at hand, wallpapered a room, painted a house. She gave them all to me.

Sunshine and rain, snowflakes.

Songs, tunes and lyrics remembered for a lifetime. Sandy beaches, shady trees, books, friends and family well loved and long remembered.

Hard times and exciting times. Disappointment and unexpected rewards. Gardens planted in many homes, walks in towns all over the world. Saying hello and saying goodbye.

Sunday school and Buddhist retreats. The blend of so many things that make up a life of 84 years and counting. Holding babies, watching them grow, feeling their love and returning it. My children, grandchildren, great grandchild. My cup runneth over with thanks and appreciation.

● ● ●

Being Tenderly Tended

It began when I was four years old. I was one of the last children in the United States to have whooping cough before the vaccine was available. Many children died of this disease. I survived, thanks to being tenderly tended by my mother and grandmother.

More than tending me, they isolated me from other children, so I would not pass the infection along, and in a way that made it fun for me. They took me fishing every day to a secluded spot on the rocks at Sheepshead Bay, not far from Coney Island. We sat in the sunshine, resting, and in my case, recovering. I did survive and did not infect others.

Many years later on my 82nd birthday, all my family came to celebrate. I could not conceal the pain I felt in my left knee.

My husband did not want me to have it replaced, as I would not be able to care for him, and he would not have strangers in our house.

When my son Bill returned home to Lopez Island in Washington State, he phoned me and said, "Babs, I can't stand to see you in pain. Make an appointment to have your knee replaced and I will be there to take care of Coot and you when you come home."

He was true to his word and gave up six weeks of his life. He brought my husband to see me every day, and at home installed bars and banisters everywhere needed.

● ● ●

Lights in the Window

To my great granddaughter:

Dear Maisie,

I can hardly wait to hold you and sing baby songs to you. Maybe Dad will accompany me on his guitar.

Dear Grandma,

I think Maisie will be swept away by our rendition of "Come Rain or Come Shine."

I was really thinking of "Rock-a-Bye-Baby" or "By Baby Bunting," but "I'm gonna love you come rain or come shine" will be good too, as I already do.

How often it is easier to express our feelings in a song or poem.

My husband seldom expressed his feelings for me orally but he could say the words to a country song by Willie Nelson, "My life has been a pleasure and it's all because of you." I love to hear that.

We are all lights in the window. How fortunate our paths have crossed here in this very room. So many times we listen and hear a thought that has been ours, expressed by someone else, and feel a kinship. It's like hearing an old familiar song.

● ● ●

Favorite Fragrance

The scent of a tangerine as you break the skin to peel it always makes me think of Christmas morning. There was always one in the toe of my stocking, and we always had to empty our stockings and eat the tangerine before we were allowed to open the other gifts.

Smelling clean sheets that had been washed and hung outside to dry.

The smell of ocean salt water on our way to the beach on Long Island.

Momma, dressed to go out, "Evening in Paris."

Orange blossoms – Florida.

Eucalyptus – California. On my first trip to California I noticed a strange exotic smell I had never smelled before. It turned out to be Eucalyptus.

Freshly cut grass

Good and clean talcum powder – babies

Lavender Provence

Any odor coming from the oven but especially apple pie, juices running over, burning on the oven floor.

● ● ●

Courage

Courage is not necessarily to go anywhere or do anything exceptional, but to do those things we already feel deeply, and to live through the consequences. Example: vote, and then support that candidate's program even if unpopular with your friends and neighbors, even your spouse, canceling out their vote year after year, and having the courage to withstand the verbal abuse because deep inside you, you felt it was right.

Probably the most courageous thing many of us do is get out of bed in the morning and attempt to have a meaningful and productive day.

As long as my husband lived my day was automatically planned: caregiving, doctor's appointments, etc. After his death I had to reimagine and reinvent my life. My daughter suggested that I plan to have some social contact every day, as well as get out and walk. I took her advice. I went back to my writing class, play bridge 3 times a week, and meet a good friend for lunch on Wednesdays. It works. It no longer takes courage to get out of bed. Life is good!

• • •

"The most beautiful form of courage is to be happy,"

To be happy is a choice. People will say, "Oh that's easy for you. That's the way you are." Not true. Happiness is a choice not a constant condition. The effects ripple and make others feel good. Perhaps we should all make a New Year's resolution to choose happiness in a time when there is so much sadness and negativity. Be brave, choose to be positive. Choose happiness.

Inheritance

Daddy gave me strong legs, a sense of humor and an outgoing personality.

Momma gave me good manners, a sense of responsibility, and a confidence that I could do anything that I wanted to do if I tried hard enough.

There were material things as well: jewelry, furniture, books; but what I mentioned first were the most important.

● ● ●

Lopez Island, San Juan Islands, Puget Sound, Washington

The trip to Lopez on a ferry crossing Puget Sound through mist and fog, and an occasional low-lying cloud, is magical. The arrival, embraced by family, so happy to have you, is equally magical.

This is what going to Lopez has always meant to me. After an absence of three years for the 4th of July, this trip was double sweet. My grandson had made me a bed, sanding every board to smooth perfection. Who wouldn't have a good night's sleep in such a special bed, with a fine mattress bought by my son to make me comfortable. Unexpected? Not really, knowing this: thoughtful and well made are the ways they express their love.

You are not leaving – even as the light fades quickly now.
You are arriving – at a place you feel comfortable in.

○ ○ ○

I am discovering things I didn't know about myself.

Some good, some bad. The ability to handle almost anything that needs taking care of: the house, the car, the garden, paying bills and taxes, endless bureaucratic nonsense. I do know when to call expert help, such as my daughter. The inability to suffer fools, cry-babies and naysayers.

And I don't.

As the light fades, there isn't time for them. There is only time for enjoying good company, good books, beauty in music, art and flowers. Walking to the ocean to watch the giant waves or serene blue water. A quiet time before dinner with a martini (2 olives, please) or a glass of wine. A phone call to a far-away friend.

○ ○ ○

I have arrived at a place where, as the light fades, I find true contentment and look forward to my next great adventure.

FLYING SOLO

Barbara Cropsey Moody

www.ingramcontent.com/pod-product-compliance
Lightning Source LLC
Chambersburg PA
CBHW050755110526
44588CB00002B/9